LEARNING TO
LOVE THE
POLITICS

LEARNING TO
LOVE THE POLITICS

>◀ HOW TO DEVELOP ▶◀

INSTITUTIONAL SUPPORT FOR ADVANCEMENT

LARRY D. LAUER

WASHINGTON, D.C.

© 2010 Council for Advancement and Support of Education
ISBN: 0-89964-427-9
ISBN 13: 978-0-89964-427-1
Printed in the United States of America

Limit of Liability/Disclaimer: While the publisher and author have used their best efforts in preparing this book, they make no representations or warranties in respect to the accuracy or completeness of the contents of this book. Neither the publisher nor the author is engaged in rendering legal, accounting, or other professional services. If legal advice or other expert assistance is required, the services of a competent professional should be sought.

Council for Advancement and Support of Education (CASE). Education's leading resource for knowledge, standards, advocacy and training in alumni relations, communications, fundraising, marketing and related activities.

CASE offers high-quality training, information resources, and a wide variety of books, videotapes, and materials for advancement professionals.

For more information on CASE or a copy of our books catalog, visit *www.case.org* or call 202-328-5900.

Book design: O2 LAB
Art Director: Angela Carpenter Gildner
Editorial Director: Julie K. Schorfheide

COUNCIL FOR ADVANCEMENT
AND SUPPORT OF EDUCATION
1307 New York Avenue, NW
Suite 1000
Washington, DC 20005-4701
www.case.org

CASE EUROPE
3rd Floor, Paxton House
30 Artillery Lane
London E1 7LS
United Kingdom

CASE ASIA-PACIFIC
Unit 05-03
Shaw Foundation Alumni House
11 Kent Ridge Drive
Singapore 119244

⇒◀ CONTENTS ▶⇐

⋙◄ PREFACE AND ACKNOWLEDGMENTS ►⋘

THIS IS NOT A KISS-AND-TELL BOOK. It is not intended to target the gremlins in the academy that make it difficult to get things done. Instead, it is intended to identify the typical problems and barriers encountered by advancement professionals and to make thoughtful suggestions for addressing those obstacles.

I will, therefore, rarely refer to specific situations, but I will attempt to identify the most typical problems I have seen in a number of institutions around the world. My suggestions for dealing with the barriers also have generally not been learned in any one place. Rather they have been abstracted from a long career that has taken me to countless organizations in many different geographic and cultural settings.

This book is based on my years as a student and on more than 40 years as a professor, academic administrator and advancement professional in higher education. Therefore, it is difficult to ascribe insights and observations to specific individuals, but I will try to give credit where credit is due.

In retrospect I must admit that virtually all of these insights I owe to collaborators in one institution or another, and to all who were a challenge to me as I tried to figure out how to get things done. As a professor, I was also a producer of media. As an academic administrator, I was also a communication consultant to business and nonprofit organizations. As an advancement professional, I collaborated and consulted with academic institutions, both public and private, all over the world. My exposure to organizational political realities has therefore been long-term and varied, and so the insights I apply here to the academy may also apply very easily to other kinds of organizations.

It's also important to acknowledge I have always been a maverick in this business. I always took the road less traveled, and so I always had to deal with political issues and serious barriers at almost every turn. I began my career academically at the instructor level, and when I asked my dean if I could be promoted to assistant professor, he said, "We better get you tenure while we can." He always said he never would fight a battle that he could not win, and that given the way I combined professional activities with teaching he was not sure I would always be able to get tenure. So at his initiative I became a tenured instructor, the only one I have ever known, and I have been indebted to that dean ever since. That gave me a foundation to deal with the politics for the many years ahead.

Of course, in the early years I was the typical complaining faculty member. This is how I found myself with the position of head of continuing education. I didn't think the university was doing what it could to serve adult students, and before I knew it I was given the challenge: "Put up or shut up." And boy did I have political issues to deal with ahead of me.

The continuing education position meant I administered the entire university after 4 p.m. and was responsible for the whole summer school and all noncredit programs—including those in business. So I found myself in an interesting relationship with the other academic administrators and deans. Clearly, I had to compete for any support I got, financial or otherwise. The time I spent on politics amazed me, and it led me to realize that I had better learn the strategy and tactics—and learn to love practicing them.

In time I moved into advancement as a specialist in communication and marketing. Strategic communication was my teaching field, so this move was a rare opportunity to be an administrative officer practicing what I had been teaching. Most university administrators are forced to give up their teaching because they cannot keep up with their academic field. What they do as administrators has nothing to do with what they were teaching. But in my case, the two went hand in hand, which has made my whole higher education adventure more meaningful.

As higher education became more and more competitive I realized we would have to become a lot more sophisticated in how we recruited students and raised money. We would have to add the subject matter of marketing to strategic communication, and it seemed quite natural for the maverick in me to approach my work in just that way. During the years I had continued teaching, I found myself integrating marketing and strategic communication, and teaching and writing about what I was learning. All along, the feeling that I was a maverick made me think that I had to keep earning my right to teach, and so I kept writing and publishing as I could. That led to several books, including one of the first to explain integrated marketing as it applies to higher education from the perspective of an insider.[1] That "insider" viewpoint eventually led to the realization that the politics of making all this work would have to be explained.

I have been particularly encouraged by the staff at CASE. Most especially I must name and thank John Lippincott, president; Rae Goldsmith, vice president of advancement resources; Norma Walker, vice president of advancement programs; and Lori Woehrle, former director of book publishing and current director of corporate relations. These leaders of the profession understand that advancement is moving front and center all over the world and that the professionals who practice it will have to understand all the issues facing the industry, as well as the politics involved with getting the job done.

Other association executives, and experiences they enabled, have produced valuable insights as well.

Terry Hartle, senior vice president at the American Council on Education (ACE) and Tim McDonough, ACE vice president for external relations, made it possible for me to have a professional development session with ACE staff, as well as perform a marketing and communication assessment.

Roland King, vice president for public affairs of the National Association of Independent Colleges and Universities (NAICU), gave me access to member presidents and communication officers in a workshop, before NAICU's annual conference, to review the basics of integrated marketing and discuss implementation problems.

Susan Chilcott, vice president of communications at the American Association of State Colleges and Universities (AASCU), gave me access to member presidents and their communication officers to discuss the issues and politics related to marketing the academy.

On two occasions in the last several years, once in Dallas and once in Washington, D.C., I met with the advancement professional members of the American Association of Collegiate Schools of Business (AACSB International) at their annual conference to discuss business school marketing as it relates to the marketing of the parent institution. My thanks to Marie Sabina, AACSB global professional development associate, for enabling the Washington, D.C., opportunity.

My special thanks to Stan R. Key, director of alumni affairs and executive director of the University of Kentucky Alumni Association, for inviting me to speak about and discuss the challenging future facing alumni programs, at the annual meeting of the Council of Alumni Association Executives (CAAE).

I believe these programs are of critical importance to the competitiveness of academic institutions, and I found my sessions and conversations with CAAE members incredibly helpful.

Kristi Hoban, associate vice chancellor for alumni relations at Texas Christian University and president of Private College and University Alumni Directors (PCUAD), invited me to lead the opening session with PCUAD members at their annual conference on the future of alumni programs. Both alumni leadership associations represent the top executives and shapers of the alumni profession, and so my discussions with them were very influential in developing my thinking.

Some time ago I had a great meeting with the members of the College News Association of the Carolinas. My thanks to Vince Moore, director of news and media relations at Furman University, for making that happen. Furman has been an innovator, under the leadership of former vice president Gregg Carroll, in integrated marketing in higher education, and its staff is clearly very experienced at successfully managing the politics.

I had an especially enlightening session with the members of the Academic Library Advancement and Development Network (ALADN), who proved very committed to becoming sophisticated in the politics of advancing their libraries. I am especially indebted to Shannon Chance, professor of architecture at Hampton University and Ph.D. candidate at the College of William and Mary; and Karlene Jennings, director of development at the Earl Gregg Swem Library, at William and Mary. Jennings chaired the conference, and Chance chaired my session.

I also want to thank Scott Sullivan, dean of fine arts at TCU; Ron Jones, dean of fine arts at the University of South Florida; and Elizabeth Cole, executive director of the International Council of Fine Arts Deans (ICFAD), for inviting me to participate with Stamats' principal consultant, Eric Sickler, in a post-conference workshop on marketing. Almost half the conferees stayed for this session, and it was an especially enlightening discussion on how "sub-brand" programs advance their individual identities while also advancing the university's brand. Dealing with this issue of program silos in academic institutions is one of the most sensitive of the political issues that we address, and working with these deans was time well spent.

Most recently I conducted two sessions at the CASE Annual Conference for Senior Communication Officers. I want to thank Brian Eckert, director of media and public relations at the University of Richmond, for the opportunity. In one session we discussed what the word *integrated* really should mean in integrated marketing, but in the other I previewed the material and suggestions in this book. I am indebted to the participants for their lively discussion and good wishes for my completing this project.

I have worked with many institutions over the last 10 to 15 years. In some cases I had a consulting relationship over a period of time, and in others my time there was mostly for professional development purposes. But in all cases the focus was on solving the problems of making marketing and other advancement activities work in a complicated political situation. I therefore want to thank former Vice President for Advancement Howard Lipman and the senior administration and advancement staff at Florida International University; former Vice President for Marketing and Communication Tom Huddleston, Associate Vice President Terry Helms, President John Hitt and the entire senior administration at the University of Central Florida; former Vice President for Advancement Sandra Conn, President Indira Samarasekera and the entire advancement staff and senior administration of the University of Alberta; former Vice President for Advancement Cassie McVeety and the senior administration and advancement staff of Portland State University; Assistant Director of University Communications Jeffrey Wakefield and the senior administration and advancement staff of the University of Vermont; President David Maxwell, the marketing and advancement staff and the senior administration of Drake University; Director of Alumni Relations Teo Choo Soo and the entire advancement staff at the National University of Singapore; and Development Officer Norma Aburto Lugo and the senior administration and advancement staff of Universidad de las Americas. There are others, I am sure, but these I especially acknowledge as having influenced my thinking.

In addition, I want to mention a week I spent in Poland with advancement officers from universities all over the country. I especially want to thank Maciej Kolasinski, director of strategy and development for the TEB Education Corporation. This was an especially helpful week that concentrated on adapting integrated marketing to international situations, but also focused on the politics of making it happen in an interesting political environment.

I want to acknowledge two associations of advancement and marketing leaders whose members have been important colleagues of mine, some of them throughout most of my career. Lamplighters is an organization of advancement leaders, many of whom are the pioneers of the field. A number of its members, most notably Michael Schoenfeld, vice president for public affairs and government relations at Duke University, have urged me to complete this book. They, more than most, know the politics of blazing the way for this field in a rapidly changing academic world. The Forum for Higher Education Marketing, a new group of advancement pioneers, is bringing together people from old and new media to address the issues before us.

Also an important force in developing my insights has been my friend Tom Hayes, professor of marketing at Xavier University, founder of the Forum for Higher Education Marketing and one of the founders of the American Marketing Association's annual Symposium on the Marketing of Higher Education. My involvement in this symposium over the years has also provided sessions where political issues have been discussed and solutions developed.

Another member of the Forum and an important collaborator of mine in marketing problem-solving is Terry Flannery, executive director of marketing and communication at American University, my alma mater. Flannery earned her reputation as a leader in our field when at the University of Maryland, and my collaborations with her since she took over the program at AU have been an important component in the evolution of my thinking.

I also want to acknowledge the role the senior staffs at ACE and NAICU are playing in my understanding of the importance of the legislative political world to our future. I include in that group a close colleague and friend, Barrett Karr, who was an important legislative aide in the George W. Bush administration and is currently the minority staff director for the U.S. House Committee on Education and Labor. Besides being a TCU alumnae and friend, she is teaching me the inside realities of government.

And my recent time in Washington has also been enriched with an ongoing dialogue with David Wheeler, executive editor of the *Chronicle of Higher Education*. Wheeler has assumed the challenge of making the *Chronicle* the premier international publication and website of higher education and sees the future of higher education from an international perspective, as do I. These conversations have meant more than I can say to my understanding of the awesome meaning of rapid change in our future.

Recently I have also enjoyed an association as adjunct fellow at the Center for Strategic and International Studies (CSIS) in Washington, D.C. In addition to enriching my teaching about international communication issues, this association has encouraged me to finish this book. CSIS Director of Marketing Karina Marshall, completing an MBA at Oxford, has been especially supportive of the project. But Vice President of External Relations Andrew Schwartz, President John Hamre and director of the transatlantic media project Reginald

Dale have become close and influential colleagues on matters of political influence in organizations and in government.

I must also acknowledge what I have learned from the critical thinking involved and political challenges of advancing the Schieffer School of Journalism. Working with CBS News icon Bob Schieffer and Schieffer School Director John Lumpkin—not to mention my work with faculty colleagues Tommy Thomason, John Tisdale, Julie O'Neil, Maggie Thomas and Mike Wood—has been a sheer joy.

In addition, my work with colleagues at TCU over the years has been what has enabled my involvement in this field from its earliest moments. From Chancellors William Tucker, Michael Ferrari and Victor Boschini, to Provosts Bill Koehler and Nowell Donovan, to all the vice chancellors and deans over the years, I must give my thanks. It has been both a challenging and rewarding ride to make it all happen in collaboration with them.

And of course the brilliance of the TCU marketing and communication staff has been the key to everything about marketing that I ever learned. Most of them have been here for most of the years I led the team and thus have played a major role in shaping much of my thinking. Tracy Syler-Jones, my trusted associate for many years, succeeded me this year to become vice chancellor. I must add here how very proud I am of this, as it is a succession plan we managed to carry out, a situation all too rare in this business. And so now Syler-Jones is doing the heavy lifting while I turn my attention to reflecting on all these years of professional development, teaching what I think I've learned and addressing some of the issues that I think will shape the future of the academy.

And finally, my wife, Sterling, has been with me from the very beginning of this wild adventure. All the lessons learned here were put into perspective through long and patient collaborations with her all along the way. She encouraged me when I was ready to quit and when I became disillusioned. She helped edit this book. There are no adequate words to express my deep gratitude to her. Indeed she has been a true life partner in every way.

I am sure I am leaving people out of this list that deserve mentioning. The very thought of this possibility pains me. But the years I have reflected upon here have been many. So suffice it to say I subscribe to the "you are what you eat" theory of communication: I am certain that the ideas that work should be credited to someone else. For the others, I'll accept full credit.

And finally, I want to thank Julie Schorfheide, book publisher and editor at CASE Books, for making this book better than it was when she received it.

NOTE

1. See *Competing for Students, Money, and Reputation: Marketing the Academy in the 21st Century* (Washington, DC: CASE, 2002). My other book, *Advancing Higher Education in Uncertain Times* (Washington, DC: CASE, 2006), discusses the fundamental changes facing colleges, universities and schools regarding new attitudes about the role of government in education, who should support education, the responsibilities of students and parents and education as a competitive industry.

⇥◄ A NOTE TO ADVANCEMENT PROFESSIONALS ►⇤

THIS BOOK IS FOR ALL ADVANCEMENT PROFESSIONALS, no matter their discipline or institution type or geographic location. Politics is politics around the world, and you'll be able to glean helpful advice for advancing your career as well as your institution throughout the text.

However, marketing—especially integrated marketing—is what I know best, and my examples are drawn from my marketing experience.

I believe that marketing is changing how communications, development and alumni relations are done. The political challenge is to get others in academic institutions to understand that premise. I hope you will join me in this effort.

Learning on the Job

EACH SUMMER a group of young professionals showing promise for an exciting future in higher education advancement gather with a group of senior professionals serving as their teachers to immerse themselves in the strategies and tactics of their fields. At the conclusion of their time together at the CASE Summer Institute, the attendees are asked about their thoughts as they return to their institutions. Inevitably two comments are heard every year:

1. "The people who really needed to hear this were not here," and
2. "If I did not have to deal with the politics, I could do a much better job of advancing and marketing my institution."

The fact is that politics is a reality of institutional life. It took me a while to accept it, but I came to learn that I would be much happier, and certainly more effective, once I embraced politics as still another area of expertise I would have to develop. And so each summer the attendees are sent back home with this admonition: "Learn to love the politics, because it will always be a major part of your job." There is no way to avoid institutional politics unless you settle for a position where you only do what you are told and where you have no ambition to use the power of your knowledge and talent to help advance your institution. Because if you want to settle for that, you will spend much of your time educating those who don't understand what you do and don't realize and appreciate how complicated it really is to do it well.

Universities are like small cities. Even the chief executive officer has limited control. While certain line administrative positions can be managed, the larger enterprise moves forward mainly through the influence of dynamic leadership. Let the faculty vote no-confidence, and the movement comes to an immediate halt.

These small intellectual cities are facing an unprecedented sea change. Competition for students, money, visibility and reputation has heated up, domestically as well as internationally. At many academic institutions, a great challenge lies in trying to educate some faculty and staff members about just how competitive higher education has become and how much that competition is changing everything. One might assume that people who make their livelihood in higher education would follow these trends, but that often is not the case.

Most academics are consumed with their research and teaching. They truly believe that the quality of what they do will, all by itself, attract the support the institution needs. Executive and staff people are often so focused on their daily tasks that, while they may have a general idea that change is coming, they do not see strong indications of it in their day-to-day work. They see no need to address pressures they do not yet feel. To do so seems premature and possibly unnecessary.

Of course, academics, executives and staff members all know that competition for students is intense. But what they may not be fully conscious of is just how informed today's consumers—students and their families—are about how the system works. More and more families have second- or third-generation college graduates in them and are no longer intimidated by the concept of selectivity. The thought that an institution may not admit them does not put off students as much as it did in the past. Students and their families today are completely aware of all the exceptions to admissions "requirements" that institutions will consider, the criteria that institutions use to make such exceptions and all the ways students might be able to negotiate for the best deal.

Indeed, these families have their own quality criteria. For many, an air of selectivity is still important, even with all the exceptions. But these families also strongly expect that "customer service" will be delivered as promised, that sports and recreation opportunities are top-notch, that classes are small, that professors are high quality, that food service meets current standards, that living environments are comfortable and that career counseling and placement is extremely professional.

And then there is the matter of financial aid. For many of these families, the fact that a son or a daughter got a scholarship, no matter how the "getting" of it was accomplished, is a big brag factor, even when the money itself is not the real issue. To put it another way: The common practice of discounting tuition in order to attract desirable students has created a financial aid entitlement mentality, even among those students who are not necessarily academic stars. How many times have I heard a prospective parent say to me, "But they offered a scholarship to her and you didn't"?

In the final analysis, the student recruitment environment has changed dramatically. Prospective families are more educated about the system and therefore are able to "shop" the institutions that they know in advance will accept their children. It is a whole new ballgame, and dealing with this situation requires new marketing approaches and much more sophistication.

The same level of intense competition has come to the fundraising arena as well. More and more organizations are asking for more and more money every day. In many institutions, multiple campaigns mean that major donors are asked for money over and over again, raising issues of a growing donor fatigue.

And, of course, it seems that every nonprofit organization in the universe is asking for annual contributions, launching major campaigns, building endowments and competing for all the available philanthropic dollars in a community. In some cities the major nonprofit institutions have to coordinate their campaigns in order to relate to the giving patterns of their funding foundations and wealthy patrons.

As the higher education world becomes more international, this competition for private money is also becoming more international. U.S. colleges and universities have been raising money abroad, following their alumni to wherever they live and work. But recently more and more foreign institutions are establishing fundraising operations in the United States—not just soliciting their alumni, but also calling on corporations and foundations with international and other interests compatible with theirs.

With so many people and institutions representing important and attractive causes asking the same people and organizations over and over again for money, what does it take to make a donor more loyal to your cause? This will be the big question of the future and the big problem to solve. These factors all involve not just new approaches to cultivating donors but political thinking and acting, inside and out.

In the midst of all these changes, governments around the world are cutting back their support and getting out of the education business to the extent that they can, except where their interests are directly served, such as in science and technology, career preparation and financial aid. More and more, educational institutions are being left to determine how to support all those other areas of intellectual and creative activity: the humanities, social sciences, the arts. Part of this governmental withdrawal is being driven by the issues pressing upon governments everywhere, but a very large contributing factor is the belief that most colleges and universities now have the capacity, through their vast alumni base, wealthy friends, connections to foundations and elaborate pricing structures, to pay more of their own way.

So what does it take to lead and manage an organization's advancement operation that has suddenly been brought front and center with a new mandate for greater levels of achievement? How do you go about planning and managing the operations when the overall organization is more like a small city than a company? How do you deal with the politics? Which issues are most often encountered and which barriers to success are most common, and what have we learned about how to deal with them?

Visibility is also more difficult to come by in this world dominated by an explosion of information. An institution no longer gets attention by just sending out press releases, which usually get lost in the information clutter. Becoming known in the world has therefore become a real strategic challenge, and the reality is that organizations of all types have to compete to be noticed.

Building a reputation from pure visibility once it is achieved is still an additional challenge. In today's world you have to ask, "Reputation for what?" And you also have to ask, "Visibility and reputation with whom and at what cost?" These questions require a strong degree of professional sophistication in figuring out how, strategically and tactically, to answer them effectively. And the strategies and tactics will have their political implication as well, both for organizations and for individuals. People have to be dealt with, differing interests addressed and deals will have to be made … even for visibility.

And so defines the educational challenge of today's professionals in all the advancement professions: marketing, communication, fundraising, alumni relations and, yes, admissions, too. Meeting these challenges requires political savvy, but political success requires educating the people you must count on about what it is that you do.

The routine of daily work, however, offers few opportunities for this kind of education to take place. How can you inform people about the sea change the industry is going through? Where are the opportunities to simply explain about how families are "shopping" institutions, no matter how prestigious they might be? When and where can you gather people so you can tell them about how the fundraising climate has changed? What will change the minds of those who still think that telling the institution's story is a simple matter and that nothing more needs to happen? How can you teach them about the professionalism required to do advancement work successfully in today's changing academic world?

The truth is that such education must be a long-term, ongoing and constant activity undertaken by today's advancement officers. And it is also essential to do the political cultivating necessary to secure support for the work. Advancement professionals must prepare elevator speeches with talking points and develop the skills needed to work such education into normal, one-on-one conversations and into meetings that are called for other purposes. Becoming an advancement champion every day is essential to success, as well as learning how to be persistent without being overbearing. You must know how to be patient on the one hand while constantly pressing forward on the other. When you learn to make "walking the institutional advancement talk" your leadership style, you will find that half your time is spent doing it, but it is that half of your career that enables everything else to happen.

This book will help you learn about managing advancement and dealing with the institutional and academic politics that go with the job. So this book is not a how-to manual about raising money or launching new alumni initiatives or using the newest technology or designing an integrated marketing program. Rather, it is about how to make all those advancement activities work in an academic institution while building internal support for doing the job right. When an aspiring director of development or director of marketing or vice president of advancement says to me, "If only I didn't have to deal with the politics, I could do my job and be happy," I say again and again, "Learn to love the politics!" It is a bridge that must be crossed if you are to be successful in today's higher education marketplace.[1]

NOTE

1. Go to Lauer's blog, *www.larrydlauer.com*, to follow his thinking about advancement and the lessons he continues to learn.

PART I

DEVELOPING YOUR SAVVY

CHAPTER 1

Universities Are Fundamentally Different

BEFORE YOU CAN LEARN TO LOVE THE POLITICS of your organization, you must first understand its ethos and the types of people you will most certainly encounter during your career.

The first thing you must recognize is this: Universities do not operate like commercial corporations, nor are they businesses. While it may be true they should be managed more in a businesslike manner, they are fundamentally different from a business.

SMALL CITIES

Universities are very much like small cities. They have a police force, streets that need repair, utilities, restaurants, retail stores, athletics teams, academic programs—and they have politics. Chancellors and presidents have a certain amount of control; but like city managers, their management control is mostly over the staff members who report directly to them. Beyond that, their "control" is a matter of persuasive influence and politics.

It would seem that if the president keeps the board happy, she will be secure in her position. And yet experience shows that more presidents lose their jobs following a vote of no-confidence from the faculty than in any other way, besides a voluntary move. Trustees will support the president when the institution is moving ahead successfully; but when the faculty become restless and combative as a group or when the vital signs of enrollment turn south, the trustees quickly attack the administration and the president. That's when trustees are most likely to demand a change. So goes the politics of academia.

Academic deans are also often hired pretty much like autonomous presidents. They are expected to build reputations for their individual schools, find enough good students and raise money. With all that responsibility on their shoulders, they are usually able to operate as if their school were a fairly independent organization. So when an advancement professional calls on them with a set of university advancement expectations, deans in most institutions are able to respond pretty much independently. So in order to get the cooperation of a dean, people in advancement (and sometimes those in the president's office as well) must demonstrate how their expectations directly advance the goals of the dean. Thus, we enter the world of institutional politics.

Then there is the faculty. Nothing like this group exists in the corporate world. Many faculty members will view themselves as individual independent enterprises. Yes, they hire on to teach courses and in most cases produce research and publications. But while they accept the teaching load their department requires, they pretty much expect to determine their own academic interests and they feel quite autonomous when it comes to participating in other activities. That would be especially true when it comes to helping find students and money.

Most faculty think that student recruitment and fundraising are jobs for other people, and they are often reluctant to help and quite outspoken about how all this external work should be done. Yet their naïveté about such matters in no way deters their outspokenness. In fact, faculty often behave as if there is nothing that professional advancement officers know that they don't already know. It can be maddening indeed for advancement folks, but it is a political fact of life, and it must be dealt with as such.

Thus, a university is more like a small city, the units inside are like independent enterprises (some of them businesslike and others not) and faculty are unique unto themselves. And the president, treated publicly in good times much like a hallowed CEO, is internally more like a city manager with a staff of people who report to him or her but with other political realities that require skills more of influence and inspiration than of management control.

THE FACULTY LIFE CYCLE

A university faculty member's life is like no other I know. I have experienced this life in all its stages, and it is a special way of making your way through a day.

A new, young faculty member has always been preoccupied with getting and holding a job, but that is especially true today. The pressure on new faculty is enormous. First, securing a position is extremely competitive. Second, getting into the profession requires some financial sacrifice. Higher salaries come only after many years, when one has acquired a visible reputation and high academic achievement (with the possible exception of some highly competitive technical fields). Third, a new colleague in the department is hit immediately with requirements for tenure, which almost always include research and publication. The younger and more inexperienced one is, the harder all this is to do.

Being a new faculty member also means living with a contract that must be renewed every year and then eventually either getting tenure or facing the world awkwardly without a job. During these first five to seven years, most faculty members feel little loyalty to their institution or any inclination to help with issues related to advancement. When you understand the circumstances of faculty members, it's easier to understand why they can seem aloof and uncaring to university staff and even come off as naïve about the realities of the larger world.

When a faculty member earns tenure, one of several typical attitudes can form. One attitude is to continue a focused loyalty to one's academic field. This very often leads to a move to another university, since academic publication and recognition lead to job offers and moving to another institution is the quickest way to a significant salary and rank upgrade.

Another attitude that often accompanies newly acquired tenure is the feeling that one finally has the freedom to enjoy the lifestyle of a university community a bit more. And this, however, can take one of two turns. The first is to stop research activities and publishing, focus only on meeting classes, teach with yellowed notes and eventually become deadwood. But the other is to get more interested and involved in the institution and its success and to eventually become involved in recruiting students, raising money and visiting with alumni clubs.

The faculty members with this attitude are the ones advancement people need to identify, and they are not too hard to spot in a faculty meeting. Once they have been found, the advancement program can be built largely on their shoulders. The others can be ignored. It is a big mistake to try to convert those who are not eager to get involved. Rather, the train can be moved out of the station just by mobilizing and energizing those eager to help. But more on this thought in a later section.

Even students rarely understand what the life of a faculty member is like. As a student I certainly didn't. I never considered becoming a teacher at any level, because what I imagined the work to be like had no appeal. It looked like a life of preparing daily speeches, coping with unpleasant pressure to publish, grading reams of papers and exams into the wee hours and dealing with problem students and irate parents. Who in their right mind would want to do this, and do it for little money and even less praise? But once I was in the world of teaching, I found a whole new experience I never anticipated. And that was the surprising experience of actually "living a subject matter."

Students come and go in four years. For them, an education seems to have a beginning and an end in that timeframe, even though we talk a lot these days about lifelong learning. The really talented teacher lives his or her subject matter constantly for a lifetime and evolves in his or her thinking all the time. Students just join in for four-year periods along the way. Having this perspective is critically important to understanding how really good professors think about their place in the university. And when professors' devotion to a subject matter is accompanied by a deep caring about the growth and success of the institution, it is possible to pull them into becoming a part of a total institutional team—one that integrates faculty and staff into the common cause of institutional and academic program advancement. It's a political task, pure and simple, and you must be prepared to orchestrate it.

THE DYNAMICS OF ACADEMIC INSTITUTIONS

Each institution is at a different point in its own development. And while universities can seem very much alike on the surface, the special characteristics of each institution's current place in its specific evolution is a large part of what defines the individual differences.

New institutions

Start-up institutions are usually driven by a strong sense of mission. New community colleges, for example, meet the critical career- and job-training needs of people in their immediate geographical area. New for-profit educational ventures generally focus on the continuing education needs of adults who seek easy, convenient access to practical, job-related instruction.

For new colleges and universities, clarity of mission is a key factor in developing a collective sense of institutional purpose, enthusiasm and teamwork. Over time, this intense focus on founding mission can fade as the institution adds new programs and initiatives to serve more and more people, and with this fading focus on mission comes a slowing of forward momentum.

Moments of strong leadership

This natural and inevitable fading of mission and focus is indeed a leadership challenge. And so another characteristic of institutional development is the surge that happens during moments of very strong leadership. Looking back and studying these moments is a useful exercise for institutional leaders. The lesson almost always will be that the really big difference does not spring from starting a new advertising campaign or hiring a major marketing firm, although these initiatives might be part of a total resurgence package. Rather, the really big difference is always made by a strong leader and his or her team. Marketing and communication materials can articulate a renewed inspirational direction and help set the tone for leadership, but it is the articulation of a renewal that starts the train down the track. And very often true, this new inspiration or direction (or vision) is not a whole new mission but a realignment of the founding mission with the realities of changes in society and market needs.

Moments of plateau

Moments of weak leadership will also occur in every institution. This happens when the university loses forward movement and finds itself on a plateau. Everything slows and eventually stops. Leaders become complacent. When challenged, they become defensive or, even worse, assume a posture of denial. During these periods, faculty and staff complaints begin to surface and gradually intensify, and morale begins to suffer. Eventually, forward movement stops completely. Enlightened leadership teams will recognize these plateaus fairly early and will regroup and launch new strategic planning activities. Soon, they will announce new major initiatives that will reactivate an emotional commitment to mission and will now articulate it as the vision.

But when current leaders become seriously defensive or have buried themselves too far in denial, the day has come for big change. New leadership must be found. When this occurs, one of two results is likely. The first possibility is that a new leader arrives with his or her own idea about what a university should be and sets out to remake this one in that image. The second is that a new leader arrives who is savvy enough to look for the institution's inherent strengths and then to gather a team to examine how to build upon what is here and to articulate a compelling new day for this great academic center.

If the first case happens, the institution is certain to remain on its plateau for a long time. Institutional dynamics are strong, and institutions will strongly resist becoming something they inherently are not. What they are at their core always connects back to the founding mission. When a new leader from another strong academic center tries to remake this institution in the image of another, the efforts just do not work.

Academics are prone to make this mistake because they have strong tendencies to define all great universities in the same way. An effort to remake an institution might result in some baby steps forward in specific areas, but reenergizing the whole place will not likely take place. There are too many people with already established commitments, too many traditions, too strong an institutional culture and too many unique program qualities that have become tied to the very fabric of the place for a total change to be possible. Starting a new organization would have to be done in a brand new place.

Institutions progress through their historical development with fits and starts, and it's essential to understand where yours is right now in order to advance it.

Employee and faculty unrest

When complaints intensify to the point of unrest and low morale, everyone's tendency is to identify specific problems and then try to fix them. But in my experience, this approach often leads nowhere. You may fix this or that problem, but morale remains unaffected overall. This is a difficult lesson. When morale is low, the fundamental problem is that the forward movement of the institution has stopped and people are restless and concerned about their future. A loss of visible, effective and convincing leadership is really at the heart of the matter.

It's funny how when the whole train starts moving again the complaints seem to go away—many of them, at least—and the tone at the institution changes dramatically. It's not that all problems have disappeared or that the more serious ones do not need to be addressed. Rather, people are feeling optimistic again because the train is moving, and the little problems take their right place in the institution's dynamics. We are on our way again, and that is what matters most. Analyzing and understanding this kind of dynamic is critical to understanding the politics of institutions and to designing your advancement strategy.

Moments of financial stress

In the life of most organizations there are periodic moments of financial hard times. When the whole economy is in stress the issues are especially perplexing. Enrollments are threatened, endowments shrink, budgets get smaller, salary raises go away and people despair.

The way in which an institution gets through these times tells a lot about its leadership and its long-term resiliency. Some institutions stay in denial too long. Others begin cutting across the board, creating a situation that can eventually weaken the whole institution. And still others ask, How can we come out of this even stronger when the crisis is over?

When you see institutional leaders re-examining mission, fine-tuning vision and vowing to preserve inherent strengths, you have a very good indication that the institution will not be crippled by the crisis. These activities require that the institution put in place organizational processes where people have a chance to learn the facts of the situation, to bring forth both their fears and their ideas and to see firsthand that they have an executive team that is on top of the situation. This is the critical factor: Does the executive team look like it knows what it's doing, and is it operating with a high degree of transparency? Because then if salaries are trimmed, budgets reduced or even programs cuts, people will see the professionalism of the leadership in action. And while they will not like the negatives that must be faced, they will at least understand that the leadership team will keep the ship floating and headed in the direction of a stronger future.

These are the times that try men's (and women's) souls, indeed, but they are also moments that can make institutions stronger if the leadership steps up and steps out in the right way. For the advancement professional these are the times to orchestrate the public understanding that this is one institution that knows what it is doing and can push ahead, trusting that the necessary support from students and donors will be there.

Building booms

Many institutions experience these moments in their history, and they indeed can be transforming. Sometimes these occur during boom times in a country's history, such as the post–World War II period in the United States, when many colleges experienced rapid growth to accommodate returning veterans. But building booms can also occur as the result of a bold, visionary strategic or master plan or as a part of an energized capital fundraising campaign. These periods can dramatically alter the collegiate experience and significantly enhance the institution's marketability.

My institution used a major building initiative to create a beautiful central campus commons that moved all our parking to the edges of campus and transformed it into a completely pedestrian, impressively landscaped, living-learning environment. This project was more than just adding buildings and beauty. It emotionally and intellectually transformed the total university experience for our students, faculty and staff by making even more real the person-centered, community-based, living-learning experience we always believed we delivered. In other words, it took the total campus educational experience element of our founding mission and aligned it with a compelling, bold new vision.

Academic recognitions

Sometimes institutions can identify moments when the institution took a major academic step up. It might be when the Phi Beta Kappa chapter first arrived or when a new honors college was created. Or it might be when a significant research project was launched or when new graduate programs were announced. It's difficult to claim new academic stature without specific events or "pegs" to hang it on.

At TCU we can identify that period in the 1950s when new buildings, new Ph.D. programs and a new Phi Beta Kappa chapter transformed the academic nature of the institution. Indeed, we can clearly see today how that historic moment brought the institution to a new academic level of recognition. And seeing that clearly today can help us find the pegs we will need to orchestrate such a moment again.

Athletics cycles

It is impossible to generalize about the role of athletics in higher education, since it is viewed differently in different circumstances. Some institutions consider athletics from the "sound mind in a sound body" perspective. At these institutions it is believed that everyone should participate in some competitive sport and that "intercollegiate athletics" is merely some of the better student athletes taking on several rival schools in a fun weekend activity. Some would argue this is how collegiate athletics began and this is how it should be everywhere. Maybe this is so.

But at most institutions today, the situation is quite different from this approach. The situation at your institution depends on its location, size and, most important, history. Over the last half-century in the United States, the fascination with serious intercollegiate athletics competition has somehow become embedded in the fabric of the history and the culture of many institutions. Indeed for many, mostly large public institutions and a few privates, athletics has become a big business.

This kind of institutional history and culture has left most schools today trying to understand exactly what their athletics program means for the long-term cultural and financial vitality of their school. The intercollegiate competition, and especially winning seasons, can earn name recognition over long distances, bring an exciting social vitality to the campus community (and even a city and a state) and create a bond that enhances loyalty, but it can also take on a life of its own with incredible salaries for coaches and never-ending facilities improvements.

Critics will charge all this costs too much and raise the question once again about what a university really exists to do. In fact, a number of politicians are looking at the "big time" programs as potential tax resources and suggesting that they may no longer be totally serving the nonprofit mission of higher education, as U.S. law requires for tax exemption. But others will just disagree, arguing that athletics has become a part of the total academic and university experience.

Understanding how all this applies to your individual institution is critical to your overall institutional advancement program (especially marketing). If yours is one of those many institutions that are historically committed to success in athletics but will cycle up and down on the winning scale, you will have to understand both your current situation and the trend line you are likely to be on in order to know the politics of the moment.

If your institution is enjoying a string of winning seasons, the advancement professionals on campus will no doubt go along for the ride. You will add more positive publicity, and your communication can be a bit more mass and less focused. But in the midst of all the hype, you also should be preparing for the inevitable down cycle. Past professional practice bears out that successful student recruitment and fundraising can continue—even in the throes of losing seasons—if you remain integrated in your thinking and practice. Otherwise the bump up in students and money may not last.

Reading the future of athletics for most institutions is not easy. Critics will predict that in time athletics will burn itself out financially, taking down a lot of institutions with it. Others will argue that while an athletics program is likely to fade in importance over time, the finances will gradually adjust and all will be just fine. And of course there are the many who think there is no way to know for sure what will happen and are happy to leave the problem to others to solve, if and when the problem arrives. For marketing and other advancement professionals, however, the critical posture to take is to read the cycle situation of your institution and do the short-term planning necessary for the ups and downs.

Institutional self-image

Sometimes we think of image in photographic terms. Pretty pictures of campuses and people will establish that positive feeling we want to create, or so we think. But practice eventually teaches that pretty pictures are just that, pretty pictures, and that a positive image is the result of something far more substantial.

Positive image has more to do with total brand identity, which is a combination of messages about institutional strengths and values, consistent constituent experience of them and the repeated communication of them in the context of consistent design elements that eventually come to stand for the brand. When all this is positive and inspirational, it establishes the foundation for a positive image.

But a really positive image is more than brand clarity alone. The institution also has to be associated with a clear vision of where it's headed and must be communicating special initiatives substantial enough to prove that it's on the move. And so a really positive image only exists when opinion leaders in priority market segments are feeling, thinking and saying: "Look at the exciting things that are happening out there!" That level of ongoing forward movement comes only from a totally integrated marketing program and from understanding the politics of orchestrating the process.

On a given day standing in the middle of campus looking around and contemplating moving this whole place forward can make the task seem impossible. The enormity of the challenge can make you feel as though nothing is working, or ever will, and that it all is crumbling around you. But feeling this is commonplace and is a part of being a leader in a complex organization.

However, a systematic analysis of where you are, a strategic approach to the politics and an integrated plan pushed ahead with patience and persistence will rescue you. Then when you stop looking around and take a minute to look back, you will begin to see just how far you've come. You can become a believer, and that will help you muster the strength necessary to press on.

STYLES OF LEADERSHIP

Academic leaders

Academics enter leadership roles from many different experiences and paths. It's not unusual these days to have at least two different paths to leadership, with several different styles.

The more traditional path has been for a scholar-teacher to take on a departmental chairmanship, which often involves minimal personnel management and administrative duties. This academic chair can move on to a dean's position based on that experience, continuing a style of being more a leader or chair of the faculty than a strategic planner or builder. Sometimes this style of dean will later become a chief academic officer and thus continue to be more a leader of scholarship than a builder, even in this high administrative position.

While many institutions maintain this faculty-to-chair-to-dean path, more and more are looking for chairs and deans who behave more like educational entrepreneurs. While it's still a bit unclear where these entrepreneurs get their training, once they are on the job they will be expected to prepare a strategic plan for growth and reputation enhancement, build enrollment numbers, find talented students and faculty, participate in raising money and compete with their fellow chairs or deans for internal resources.

In this more businesslike atmosphere—especially in the highly competitive world of professional schools—issues related to faculty governance, tenure and adjunct appointments are being re-examined: How much does (or should) the faculty influence administrative decisions? How important is tenure and how rigid are its requirements? What is the role of the adjunct professor?

Helping chairs and deans adjust to this new managerial orientation can be a role for the marketing professional, if that help can be done with real savvy. In other words, by listening to problems and issues first and by helping find solutions through collaboration, you can facilitate the education necessary for chairs and deans to be successful. That indeed will be a political success.

These two paths—faculty chair and manager—tend to produce one of four types of leaders: autocratic, participatory, collegial and insecure.

The autocrat. This traditional "boss over subordinate" leader is found in all types of organizations, even academia. In many situations, academics fall back on this top-down style because, without management education or experience, they overcompensate for their insecurity by becoming directive. Some people who were the most accessible of teachers become the most autocratic of managers when they first feel the immense stress of the responsibility. This person sees control as security and subconsciously concludes that collaboration will lead to chaos.

The participatory leader. This person is either trained in management and knows how it works or has carried over participatory inclinations from academic experiences and has learned how to apply them to management situations. Either way, this approach proves in practice to be more efficient than anticipated and usually succeeds in getting enough people on the same page to move the institution forward.

The collegial leader. This potentially destructive leadership style involves an academic person who never ceases to be the teacher-scholar. The collegial leader (more aptly known as the collegial non-leader) finds it impossible to facilitate meetings that resolve issues and thus cannot make hard decisions. These leaders carry traditional faculty governance philosophy to the extreme, and the result is a situation where work units or departments are expected to settle everything on their own. In these situations, the institution never moves forward, and morale declines. These leaders think that the faculty governance approach will make them likable and supported by the faculty, but the opposite usually happens. The departments in question, and even the institution itself, can lie dormant without inspiration, and the collegial leader ultimately is criticized for being weak and indecisive.

The insecure leader. This style is actually an extreme version of the first. Some academic leaders just find themselves in over their heads when it comes to administration. They don't know what to do and feel panicked. They don't quit, however, because they come to like the position and the perks that come with it. I have seen people who were wonderful faculty members develop an insane desire to be a dean or an academic provost. Once they have the title and hear themselves called "dean" or "provost," they can't imagine life without it. They like going to the country club better than they thought they would; they get used to their higher salary and their university car. They create for themselves a state of denial about their own effectiveness. All too often these people last much longer than they should, and the university makes no real programmatic progress.

Obviously, understanding what leadership style you are working with will determine the politics of your game. With autocratic leaders your strategy is to find others who are more process-oriented and bring them together into a task force or committee. Then by ignoring the autocrat you inspire the task force members to start moving the place forward with their collective enthusiasm. With participatory leaders you celebrate and involve them in your planning. You can involve collegial leaders in your processes but cannot rely on them for help or strong response. And with insecure leaders you cannot count on anything. So here you very much have to put the process together without them.

It's important to not let yourself be stopped because a problem person is a dean or even an academic provost. Progress will take more time, but it's not impossible. You begin by ignoring the problem people, no matter who they are, and moving forward with those who will move with you. Don't waste your time trying to convert the negatives. You will find the train will move forward when your task force starts to function.

Presidential leaders

The styles of leadership just described can apply to presidents as well. But I also think of presidents in a slightly different way when I analyze how they fit into my strategic integrated planning framework. I have encountered each of these presidential types in my visits to many institutions around the world: the visionary, the elite academic, the corporate head, the consensus seeker, the relationship builder and the church leader.

The visionary. This type of president is the most exciting. This person is entrepreneurial in inclination, has a drive to make a difference, is able to articulate a vision that is anchored in the institution's founding mission and is a bit impatient about getting the place moving. He or she understands the need for participatory processes but won't let the talk go on too long. The visionary has a knack for hearing and assimilating ideas so that when the time comes to make a decision, it is articulated in such a way that most people hear some of their ideas and can embrace it. Visionaries benchmark the competition, not to copy them, but rather to differentiate from them and sail past them. Winning is paramount, but it is done by changing the game, not by attacking the opponent.

Working with this leader is a joy for the advancement professional. Designing integrated processes, determining reputation-building initiatives, doing needed research and launching new and creative programs is second nature for this type of leader. Most of them are looking for someone in their administration to work hand-in-hand with them. An effective political strategy for working with a visionary president is to quickly get into collaborative conversations and offer to help this leader achieve big goals.

The elite academic. This person got to the presidency because of academic and/or research accomplishments, often in the scientific or medical world. Thus, the person possesses the quantitative skills to watch over budgets and finances, but may (or may not) possess inspiration and creative abilities. Some of these leaders are beloved for their achievements and personalities, and others are stuffy and aloof—but many are able to maintain their status for fairly long periods through their elegance and social attitude.

This type of leader is more complicated for the advancement professional to analyze. Some will welcome a collaborator who can make up for weaknesses in the group process category or in strategic planning experience. But others might find the thought of marketing's influence on advancement and the institution as too commercial or even offensive to an academic community. The political strategy is to quickly assess where this leader stands and to offer an organized program you will be glad to manage—or, if necessary, to begin revising your résumé and looking for another job.

The corporate head. This person came from a corporation, has business experience or for unknown reasons just assumes a business-officer approach to the position. This president will most likely also have some of the visionary's qualities but will combine them with a more hard-nosed, by-the-numbers approach to decision making. Often this person will have more of a financial-officer orientation and give lots of responsibility to the CFO. The visionary might see institutional leadership as more art than science, but the corporate head will see it as science, and only possibly with an artistic spin.

This leader can also be good for the advancement professional. There will be more budget building and accountability than with the visionary, but there should also be an appreciation for integrated processes and aggressive marketing. The political strategy is to offer to help the person reach big goals and to also help with the planning. A marketing-oriented advancement professional from any of the disciplines can become a key person on this leader's executive team.

The consensus seeker. A desire to find collective agreement drives this person's style, so group process is second nature. Although this is great news for the advancement professional, the problem here might be finding ways to keep processes from taking on a life of their own and bogging down forward movement. Even in integrated marketing the talking can go on too long. Key to success with a consensus seeker is to orchestrate processes so that everyone has a say but the moment to act is not lost. The consensus seeker needs help in knowing when to act and even sometimes in how to act. Political caution needs to be exercised when going about this, however. The president must always look like the leader. ("Mr. President, I believe we can reach a conclusion from these discussions. Would you like me to put together some talking points for you?") Political strategy sometimes is simply a matter of developing the empathetic savvy to recognize the moment. This is done with practice and by just being conscious of the leader's need for it.

The relationship builder. This style resembles that of the consensus seeker. For both types, bringing people together is important. But the difference between these two types of presidents is that the relationship builder is most oriented to external or non-management-team audiences. This leader enjoys building personal relationships with alumni, donors, students and selected faculty. With this leader, long-term fundraising and student recruiting success is usually quite high. And it's possible for this type leader to be successful overall in the academy.

The marketing professional will be called on to help this leader demonstrate a substantive grasp of higher education issues. Consensus builders get their substance from participating in enriching processes, but the relationship builder must rely on the marketing and communication professional to provide that substance.

The church leader. Religiously affiliated institutions often have presidents who come from church leadership. Their management and leadership inclinations vary significantly. Some have more of a management bent than others. Some continue to be mostly spiritual leaders. Some come from denominations that seek to advance their ideology though schools and universities. Others are leaders of institutions that were historically founded by a denomination but are no longer governed or in some cases even influenced by it.

As with the other presidential styles, the more processes- or corporate-oriented the leader is, the better the advancement person will track. But often a strong connection with the church will be required. The political circumstance here is defined by the nature of the church relationship with the institution and the way the president sees that relationship. You either are aligned with it or you aren't.

BARRIERS TO MARKETING

In addition to the differences of the academy as an organization and the kinds of leadership we find there, practice suggests several typical barriers that require a bit of strategy to overcome.

Build it and they will come

I was interviewing a political science professor at a small private university in Iowa who expressed strong skepticism about the need to market universities. His scholarly expertise was political campaign communication, and he studied the subject in the Iowa caucuses. Even so, he argued that building a strong university alone would attract good students and enhance its reputation, and he didn't see advancing either one as necessary.

Here we had an academic who taught the ins and outs of marketing political campaigns and still did not see a need to translate the knowledge he gained to advance his beloved higher education. When I asked him if he thought campaigns should stop marketing their candidates' strengths because it might be cheapening his field, he thought it was a silly question and went on to explain the sophistication of the competition, of polling and of the realities of today's politics. It was clear that he had never thought much about the competitive nature of his own industry and how it was not necessary to commercialize higher education in order to make it better understood. As hard as it was for me to believe, here was an academic expert in communication who couldn't seem to grasp the idea that viewing marketing as a way of thinking would enable the development of strategies that could make his institution better understood in an increasingly complex society.

However, when I made the simple analogy between his subject matter (campaign communication) and his industry (higher education) and pointed out that we were talking about applying a way of thinking to strategic planning that simultaneously considered program development, pricing, delivery of instruction and communication, he instantly understood. So the political challenge in dealing with most faculty members is pretty much a matter of finding opportunities to carefully explain this simple truth: Marketing higher education is a way of thinking, not commercializing.

We can't just give them what they want

Another faculty member argued that the problem with marketing was that we use research to find out what students want, then promise to give it to them. He wanted to make the case that prospective students have no idea what they need and they will only find that out when they get to college. He was under the impression that we would be telling prospective students and parents that the faculty would be giving the students what they asked for, and he found that thought offensive. His assumption was that we operated from the premise that the customer was always right, and that students and parents were customers.

I explained that such research only allows us to make a connection and to find out what needs the student and his or her parents are feeling. If we can connect with them based on understanding those needs, students will come to the institution and discover, with the help of the faculty, a whole new world of possibilities.

I sometimes use the analogy of buying a car. Even though this is a commercial example, I have found that everyone can relate to it. The salesman asks you what you want in a car, and you give him a list of your needs. He then shows you one that meets those needs. But this one also has features you never considered before, mostly because you didn't even know they existed. Once exposed to these new options, however, your whole idea of what is possible in a vehicle enlarges. This is how I discovered my "need" for windshield wipers that automatically come on when it rains and adjust their own speed. And so it is with the university experience. Again, a simple explanation cautiously delivered can take care of this faculty complaint.

Marketing is too commercial

When marketing is confused with publicity and/or retail sales, the academic concern is that the university campus will be turned into what amounts to a shopping center. The fear is that everything becomes a product to be sold and students will be seen as only consumers. What reinforces this fear is when the print advertising looks too commercial or television spots look like MTV. But while today's young people and their parents expect academic institutions to demonstrate media savvy and to look like they understand the world in which they are operating, they do not expect a university to look like Home Depot and they do not expect a university to present itself as a reality TV show. Rather, marketing is a matter of making the connection between people living in a new-media world and the opportunities of a total university experience. When the advertising and communication materials look like they should, most academics end up feeling proud to see their university presented out there just as they see it.

I had the delightful experience to run into one of our education faculty members and to have her say how much she enjoyed our spot on a recent football telecast. This faculty member is never reluctant to criticize and the spot was fairly high tech, but it stressed the emotional satisfactions of the total university experience, and she could relate to it.

The internal political strategy here is to make sure your advertising reflects what you learned about your institution from research and makes you look professionally competent in this new media world. It presents your vibrant and substantive academic institution in a savvy, new-media way.

Everyone is a marketing expert

There is something about marketing and communications that makes it seem very simple to everyone else. Somehow other people think the solution to a visibility problem or an admissions shortfall is always more communication. Someone else, they think, is responsible for not giving them enough attention (which to them usually means getting more stories in the newspaper), and of course they always know exactly what that someone else should do. They can't fully embrace marketing or communication as a complex profession.

This is the constant nightmare most marketing professionals have to cope with, and it can drive some of them to leave their chosen field. It's hard for many university program heads to imagine they would actually consult with this professional, as they would with a lawyer or a doctor, so that their program might prosper. Rather, most heads of programs think that since they know their own business, they also know everything about how to communicate it.

They have no conception that marketing and communication tools, if properly used, are powerful enough to literally transform entire institutions.

The political solution to this barrier only comes with a track record of successful interactive collaboration over time and your own strategic plan to educate your colleagues. Marketing and communication professionals must demonstrate that before we write a press release or brochure or manage an event, we all need to sit down and imagine what a comprehensive plan will look like. This is the necessary process through which program people come to see just how powerful integrated approaches to marketing can be and just how professional the people are who know how to implement them. Educate by doing it is the only solution.

Other program heads as "little presidents"

This situation will be referenced elsewhere in this book as it applies to academic deans. It directly relates to the silo effect, which is one of the most significant consequences of universities being like small cities and the most significant potential barrier to getting everyone on the same brand identity page. Deans are often hired with a set of expectations that result in their behaving quite independently, and when you understand how this comes about it's easier to understand how to relate to it. But the perception that "I am the master of my own domain" often also occurs with other program directors.

Deans of admission often feel the same way. They are professionals hired to bring in a class, and they work under enormous pressure to do so. So don't try to tell them their job, which obviously is largely one of marketing the institution to prospective students and parents. Yet it's absolutely critical that a marketing and communication staff be effectively integrated with admissions.

The key is for admissions and M&C professionals to sit down and collabo-rate on a comprehensive plan. It's critical to acknowledge quickly and deeply that both the admissions and the M&C folks are marketing professionals and that each and all are eager to enhance the success of the others. This should be done before any M&C writers and designers begin work on materials or design ads. Everyone has to be on the same message points and have the same branding standards in mind before any creative work begins. When this sense of team-work is established, the work can begin. And it should be done in two parts.

The first part is the basic admissions recruitment game plan and the pro-duction of all the materials that support it. The second part is where critical potential problems can be identified and special initiatives designed to address them over and above daily recruitment activities. Such problems might be the detection of a "soft response" in a city that has heretofore been strong or growing complaints that the university is not visible enough in that city. Emerging issues such as these can be addressed by M&C through action teams and special, focused marketing initiatives.

With an ongoing integrated marketing operation, recruiting activities continue uninterrupted and periodic marketing problems are addressed at the same time. It all happens with everyone on the same page, knowing what each person is doing.

Full acceptance of integrated marketing by admissions people comes only after they experience proof of how effective it can be. I always advise the M&C director to tell the admissions dean right up front that nothing will be produced or acted on without his or her approval, and then to include that person in all deliberations about research and brand clarification. It is also critical to make the point that the integrated process is in no way intended to tell admissions what to do; rather, it's a way to expand the team's problem-solving resources.

Student affairs and marketing

The professionalization of student affairs is a good-news bad-news proposition for marketing and communication.

The good news for institutions that want to deliver a total university experience is that today's student affairs professional is clearly upgrading the out-of-classroom experience of students. Student organizations are better supported with highly professional staff and other resources, first-rate leadership programs involve students in vital community activities and services, top-quality career placement centers are far more professional than in past years, recreation activities are more state-of-the-art, health centers are better equipped, counseling centers are more engaged in serious student mental health issues and discipline is more competently handled. So then, what's the bad news?

All this professionalism has resulted in two issues for marketing and communication professionals. First, the professional directors of these programs often take on all the silo issues and attitudes discussed above. They tend to think that all they need is more communication and that someone else is to blame when they don't get the extra communication. When each director decides he or she needs a separate logo or unique brand identity, the university can be turned into a graphic diversity nightmare.

Indeed, most department or program heads have no awareness of how cluttered the university begins to appear when every student organization and student affairs program has its own logo—which, of course, each new group of students will want to change. The nightmare really begins when the M&C staff members become the logo police and end up on the defensive everywhere they go. And this can rub off on the students, too, whose leaders are working closely on a daily basis with the student affairs staff.

The second issue arises when the students or their organizations get into controversial areas. Many issues don't seem so controversial to the student affairs staff members who work with the students every day, but these issues will be controversial to alumni, donors and other external publics. The ideal solution would be for the student affairs staff to give a heads-up to M&C professionals and to initiate the formulation of issues management plans. The complex city-like nature and size of universities and daily demands on time make this difficult, however.

My experience suggests that the only long-term solution here is to design a collaborative planning process, and it must begin with cooperation between the M&C official and the vice-president of student affairs. It certainly should be possible for M&C and student affairs professionals to hold an occasional retreat to anticipate and clarify potential controversial issues and seek collaborative solutions.

It is in such a setting that the M&C director could also review the subject of brands and sub-brands and show how decisions are made about which internal departments and programs can justify a sub-brand identity. Some brainstorming can then occur about which units have a need to market to a unique market segment and which do not. For those that qualify, it can also be demonstrated how a sub-brand can be designed that also carries the institution's brand identity.

And so the politics once again lie in making the time and place to collaborate and being prepared to teach the subject matter of branding and the power of integrated approaches. But the teaching needs to be done clearly and in concise interactive briefings in settings where such interaction and collaboration is possible. Most of the time those settings must be orchestrated, for when the teaching is attempted out of the blue in a regular staff meeting, it usually falls on deaf ears or it ends up just being pushed aside and forgotten.

A DIFFERENT KIND OF PLACE

If you can grasp the idea of a university as a collection of independent entities, it quickly becomes more clear what the political challenges are going to be in trying to make it function as an orchestrated whole. Faculty see themselves as independent of management control, academic deans and department heads often think of themselves as masters of their separate kingdoms and even other administrative department directors can consider themselves as being away from central management and operating independently on a day-to-day basis. Bringing them together into an integrated approach to advancement is a matter of understanding and implementing group process and developing political skills.

It also becomes clear why so much time and effort must be devoted to these skills. When you think about spending all that time in activities you never thought about before, you might be tempted to conclude it can't be done—and that is why it often isn't done. But when you decide you won't be deterred by those who throw out the barriers, and then you learn the political skills you will need, the job indeed can be done—and done quite successfully. You just have to be willing to accept that the politics will take half your time and that you really can and will come out ahead.

Somehow, no one ever told you all this in school. But believe me: After a few months the train will start pulling out from the station, and you will be able to look back and see not only how far you have come, but also those you left standing on the platform.

CHAPTER 2

What Organizations Can Do to People

MANY OF THE POLITICAL ISSUES WE FACE IN ORGANIZATIONS are related to dealing with people in administrative positions. Some are on the top executive team; some are heads of both academic and other programs and projects. Much of your challenge will be to understand how these people think as they discharge their responsibilities.

How do these administrators see their roles? What do they believe to be their own professional strengths? What kind of professional advice will they seek? Even more important, what kind of advice will they be willing to accept? The situation is made more complicated by understanding that it's difficult to know how people will actually behave once they are in a job. Often the job changes the person in surprising ways, and this seems especially true in academia.

Having real accountability for the first time can have a surprising impact on individuals. I remember my first day on the job as director of continuing education. I walked into my new office and was suddenly terrified. The job had all seemed so simple when I was an assistant professor complaining about the administration, but now that I was actually one of them I suddenly realized I would be visibly accountable for everything I did. And so, much to my surprise, I became terrified.

In fact, it quickly got so bad that I actually experienced a mysterious force pushing me back as I walked toward the administration building each morning. The closer I got to my office, the more nervous I became. I faced more problems than I had ever imagined. First, I had complained about what we paid adjuncts, but now I controlled the budget and could do very little more with it. I had thought we needed to expand course offerings, but now realized that I was responsible if the courses didn't make their enrollment. I had been very critical of what I perceived to be a lack of marketing of the program, but now I had to figure out how to get more visibility using the same amount of money, and it was next to impossible. What was I going to do? And what made it worse, one of my so-called friends quipped in public and in my presence that I had sold out to the enemy.

That was in 1974, and I have had administrative responsibilities, academic and non-academic, ever since. And I am still standing. But it took a long time and lots of very hard lessons learned to get comfortable with the realities of administrative leadership and what it actually takes to make it work.

This experience has given me an uncommon empathy for deans trying to build their schools, provosts trying to adjust to a whole new world of major responsibilities and presidents getting used to the pressures of political life. I know how they feel because I was an academic administrator at an earlier time in my career.

Even so, dealing with the situations faced by administrators can still surprise and frustrate me. Here are some of the mental conditions I have observed in myself and others.

PARANOIA

This pervasive organizational disease is experienced by almost everyone in positions of responsibility at one time or another. It is felt by people at every level. Its symptoms include thinking the following:

- A colleague is undermining you with the boss.
- He or she is out to get your job.
- You are being badmouthed when your back is turned.
- You are being ignored by the higher ups.
- Your work is being claimed as the work of someone else.

Most of the time you are imagining these things. But not always.

When the person thinking these things is you, and even if your concerns turn out to be warranted, staying focused on keeping the train moving is your best tactic. Either way, truth or not, the fix always will be in staying the course, because in time, all these issues sort themselves out (even if, right now, it seems impossible to set straight). Besides, just thinking about it makes you mad, and you can't do your job if you are angry. The key to survival is to consciously know that all these feelings are natural, that everyone else experiences these moments too and that even your detractors will get out of the way of the train when you get it moving down the tracks.

When the problem person is someone you are trying to influence, the best tactic is a bit more direct. In this case, you should work to make sure that the person feels secure working with you. You should not show any of your own paranoia about the situation, but rather you should defuse the situation with assurances of your honest intent. Make an extra effort to reinforce your commitment to the person's best interest and let the person know that you really want to make him or her successful just as much as you want to move the institution forward.

The bottom line here is to convince yourself that you need not worry about other people making trouble for you, even when they may be trying to undermine your success. They will either shoot themselves in the foot trying or you will outlast them by staying on track and being persistent. Staying on track and being persistent, as well as being uncommonly patient, is the key to long-term survivability and success.

BEING UNPREPARED

Far too often people in academia get to positions of responsibility completely unprepared for the job. Faculty members who have never been department chairs sometimes become deans or provosts with no administrative problem-solving skills or budget management experience. Or people talk themselves into administrative positions never having worked in an academic setting before. In either case, the person is in over his head for some time (and tragically, sometimes forever), and it's hard to predict how this mismatch will affect his behavior. This is especially hard to acknowledge and deal with if this person turns out to be you.

In some cases people in these situations become very tentative and shy away from making any decisions at all. Their approach is to let problems solve themselves, or to expect others just to work things out. This can be maddening, because programs, and even entire institutions, can stop forward movement during these times and become stagnant and in disarray.

One approach to dealing with this situation is to create a study-action team to assess a program's marketing and other advancement needs and ask this person to participate in the group. Your objective here will be to first get this person comfortable in the setting and then lead the group toward making action recommendations. This can work because now the person feels more secure in knowing that the action is a group decision and that the group will share in the accountability for results.

In other cases some unprepared people in positions of responsibility compensate for their lack of confidence by actually being overassertive. In reality they are uncertain about what to do but seek to hide that fact by being autocratic. They actually become the kind of person they may have hated before they had the job. Sadly, they might never realize what's actually happened to them.

Obviously, if you can get this type of person to agree with your plan, your particular advancement program will move ahead. But if you cannot, moving to form a larger study-action team is a possible tactic to try here as well. Ask the person to participate on the team and use the energy of the group to move toward a recommendation. Usually, insecure managers behave in a controlling way in their own office, where the setting is conducive to their control. Outside their office, however, they are usually more timid and are more likely to go along with a group recommendation.

FINDING THAT FRIENDSHIPS CHANGE

One of the most difficult consequences of acquiring new administrative responsibility is that friendships can change. This event is rarely anticipated, but the change can be abrupt and surprisingly complete.

Before you or the other person had positions of responsibility, your friendship could easily tolerate differences of opinion. In fact, you might have actually enjoyed a relationship based on academic disagreements. You understood what it meant to "agree to disagree." But now your disagreements can affect things that you feel strongly about or projects that are important to your professional success. Your administrative positions have put you in completely different places, and these places represent different organizational and professional vantage points. It can become almost impossible for each of you to see the other in this new role, with these new responsibilities and powers. Sometimes this dynamic is so strong that people become adversaries and stop seeing each other completely. They may even find themselves arguing about almost every organizational issue. It's a sad reality, but a common one.

Friendships do not need to end. Knowing about this possibility may help you and others work to prevent it. Legislators today are thinking back to the days when it was possible to disagree on political issues and problem solving and still be friends at the end of the day. Perhaps that kind of statesmanship is possible in organizations, too, with some effort. And later on, adversarial friends can reconnect and find each other when their circumstances change.

Dealing with this kind of change is part of the burden of leadership and can be difficult to get used to, mostly because it is so surprising to most of us. It can be especially true in a presidency, where the adage "It's lonely at the top" seems especially apt. On the other hand, any one of us who attains a position of some responsibility will experience this loneliness to some degree somewhere along the way. It's a fact of organizational life.

HIDING BEHIND SMOKESCREENS

Many people in authority consciously or unconsciously find ways to duck out of dealing with complicated problems head on. They hate to confront difficult situations or people, and they find ways to avoid this unpleasantness. Instead of dealing directly with you (or whatever the problem happens to be), they will create an aura of being interested, and then never act.

Some managers will listen and nod their acceptance, but never actually respond. Later, you realize that nothing is happening. These managers will tell you what a great idea you have, and you feel encouraged—but nothing happens. Or they throw out a barrier such as "the trustees just won't go for it," when they really mean they just don't want to accept responsibility for it themselves. You feel paralyzed by the situation: You cannot act until you have their approval, or at least their concurrence.

But the truth is you probably can act. When a person in authority behaves this way, he or she will rarely pay attention to what you do later. If this manager gives you a smokescreen response, you should consider building a few allies around you on this issue and then use the weight of the group to move ahead. Remember: The person never said no, he or she just did not respond. So when you do move, this person will either say, "Don't do that again" or will still give no response. Again, when things are moving ahead, you are almost always on solid ground.

COPING WITH UNRELIABLE MANAGERS

A manager who says "I'll take care of it" and then doesn't is exhibiting one of the most devastating of bad management traits. You will encounter this type frequently. Managers who promise action usually do so to look efficient and cooperative, but a fear or unwillingness to act will keep them from completing the task. It's even possible for this type of manager to willfully forget his or her promise to act and subconsciously hope it all will go away or fix itself. But you or the other person involved in this situation have just had the responsibility to act taken away into another office, and so now you don't feel you can do anything.

This is particularly problematic for any advancement professional working on a project related to important timing. Once the person says "I'll take care of it," it's almost impossible to proceed. After this happens the first time, however, it's important to recognize that, with this person, it's likely to happen again and again. So your strategy is to not let that kind of conversation take place. In the future when you want to move something ahead that involves this person's area of responsibility, it's best to find a way to assemble a small group to advise you. Then, using the implied support of the group, quietly move ahead and gently inform the person about what you are doing while you are putting the project in motion.

This approach sounds a bit manipulative, but the person involved is not likely to respond. The reason this person did not act to begin with was that he or she did not know how to act, was afraid to act or did not want to bother with the project. Once you have your project under way, this person is likely to go along with the outcome and probably will never say a thing about it. If you look around, you are likely to find that this person is doing the same thing to many others and may even have a reputation for it.

BECOMING A THREAT

This is the most difficult organizational problem that talented people confront. In any career, people think that the more effective they are, the more they will be rewarded. Unfortunately, that rarely happens. This can be maddening.

And it's difficult to understand. An objective analysis would argue that the better you perform, the better your boss looks. Most people will readily agree. But the actual drama can play out differently. The paranoia factor is at work. Intellectually, your boss knows that your performance makes him or her look good, but emotionally she doubts that others are really seeing it that way.

I remember a time when, as director of communication, I was elected volunteer president of a theater board of trustees. I returned to campus thinking my boss would be extremely proud of my achievement. After all, part of my responsibility was community relations, and I now was in a position to bring new visibility to the university in the arts. Instead my boss responded by saying, "That's nice, but it's your job to get me elected to such offices." I was devastated. From that day on I worried about losing my job, thinking that everything I did was supposed to advance my boss more than the university—and I certainly should not be advancing my own career, as that would be seen as self-serving.

In time that person left the university and my career made progress. The hard lesson I learned, however, was that I would have to look for a job, rethink my role for a while or wait for my boss to move on. Since he did leave, I stayed. But I also continued to run into this situation at different levels of the institution and have had to work through it for most of my career. As usual, the best tactic is to make sure your support coalitions stay active and keep the train moving down the track. This is an important situation to think long and hard about, and it is part of the politics of administrative leadership.

One more caution: Don't let yourself be that person who feels threatened by people around you. We all have the tendency. It begins as a subconscious discomfort when you have talented people reporting to you, and that subconscious feeling of threat can influence your behavior without your even being aware of it. First you tell the person not to talk to the president without your permission and presence, and then you block a move to give that person a major project to manage. You tell yourself that the person is not ready yet or that you are the better person to handle it, when the truth is you feel threatened by this person's talent. And somehow you find yourself losing sight of the fact that maybe if you cut this person loose, she would make you into a hero.

Never forget to hire the most talented people you can find, develop them and assemble the team you know can put your institution on the map. Put the best talent out front, and help them with their careers. It will work out in the end. The better the team plays, the more the coach is rewarded. You know that now, and don't forget it.

So when you become a threat to your boss or others, remember that your approach will be to pull back and form coalitions to keep your program on track. Then you will look for a job or wait for your boss to move on. When you are the boss, you will never ever forget that the more talent you have around you, the better off you will be. Even when one of those talented people is trying an end run around you, you will find that the coach is always the coach in the eyes of everyone else.

One more thought: The best thing you can probably do for that end-run person is to pull him aside and let him know that his approach won't work and that if he has real talent you will help him succeed. Tell him that you will give him recognition when he earns it and that you will help him move up here or elsewhere when the time comes. That is the way this should work, because it's all about talent.

Sometimes people take on administrative responsibility because they are truly driven to make a difference. I have come to believe that some of us get that drive early in our lives and may never even know why. When that is the case, it's critical to understand all these lessons about administrative roles, changing friendships and talented teams. The dynamics of organizations become your reality, and you find yourself living an odyssey. You must gather talent around you, focus on realizing a vision and press ahead with persistence and patience.

Once in a while you must also step outside your organizational world and remind yourself that real friendships are based on factors unaffected by the strange dynamics of organizational leadership. Family relationships are based on different factors, too. And make no mistake: To be successful with organizational responsibility and maintain your sanity over the years, you will also need family and social friendships; otherwise you will burn out and may lose your way.

CHAPTER 3

Mastering the Political Tools

IT SEEMS OBVIOUS THAT IF POLITICS IS HALF OR MORE of organizational life we should be making some effort to teach professionals about it. So we now turn to the tactics no one probably taught you in college. (Actually, you might have been able to learn some of the interpersonal aspects of the subject matter in kindergarten, but no one told you to pay attention there either.)

Your biggest hurdle now will be to get beyond the realization that you will have to spend an inordinate amount of time developing these political skills. You will have to learn how to think strategically and how to design and implement the necessary processes, interventions and tactics to address the problems you encounter.

This chapter will discuss the use of these process tools in dealing with the many political barriers and attitude problems that advancement professionals have to address in the course of their daily work. My examples draw upon my years in higher education and my experience working with all the areas of advancement.

ACCOUNT EXECUTIVE APPROACH

My experience as a consultant and professional staff developer at many institutions of all sizes and types has convinced me that more often than not the best way to integrate departmental and school silos, get everyone on the same message page and coordinate and focus marketing and other initiatives is to develop a centralized office that functions much like an internal marketing agency. In other words, it is an office with professionals who think of themselves as account executives who confer with academic and other programs as clients, rather than an office that exists to produce materials on demand.

This approach begins with an account executive call on a client for the purpose of developing a comprehensive communication and marketing plan that clarifies that unit's distinct brand identity but also ties the unit's identity to the overall institutional identity. Such a plan will also identify the unit's target market segments and the appropriate media and other tactics to employ for each segment. The advantage of this approach is that the central office shares both planning and implementation with each unit and people in both offices are involved in getting the tactical work done. This kind of shared approach both increases the manpower and mobilizes a collective commitment to getting results.

The political aspects of the account executive's work arise when misunderstandings about the nature and role of integrated marketing are articulated or encountered or other implementation barriers appear. Barriers such as mistaking marketing for commercial publicity or fears about losing autonomous control of academic programs require education about what integrated marketing and advancement really are all about. And here is where the account executive armed with a lesson plan about the basics of integrated marketing and advancement has been made ready to respond.

Within the context of staff meetings, as well as one-on-one interviews, it is clearly possible to teach clients what they need to know about marketing and advancement in order to set aside most of their concerns. There always will be those who won't go along, but the train can move ahead without them, so long as they are not in the majority. That is where strategic thinking applies.

For example, sometimes this effort becomes a long-range project, where marketing or advancement is taught in smaller modules as a part of interactive conversations over a period of time. The key here is that the account executive has his or her lesson plan in hand and is working through it, whether or not the client is even consciously aware this is happening.

Systematic education is a powerful political tool. In the real world of politics, an ambitious political candidate uses polls to find out what constituents want to hear and then builds the campaign around telling them just that. Politicians rationalize that they must get elected before they can do good things; but once elected, real governing leadership will require that they educate constituents about the practical realities of fixing problems and the time it takes to get things done. This requires preparation and a patient and persistent systematic approach. In the case of integrated marketing and advancement, it requires seeing and communicating very basic concepts in the context of basic subject-matter categories.

THE TASK FORCE

A university-wide task force can be an effective political tool when commissioned by the president and then chaired by the head of communication and marketing. Once such a task force is put together with the president's charge to coordinate institutional message and implement new marketing activities, that group becomes an ideal forum for teaching the fundamental concepts of marketing, integration and advancement to people who can help spread the word. It also can help with political issues as well.

When kicking off a task force, regular meetings are always scheduled over a fairly long period in order to address the charge and to get the ball rolling. So if the basic subject matter has already been divided into short modules, it is pretty easy to go over some of these modules as a brief part of each meeting. And if this practice is carried out over a period of several months or a year, task force members learn enough in time to help explain it to others. So the more informed they become, the more skilled at implementation they become as well.

As these task force members commission research initiatives and digest the findings, they come to see the competitive advantage of the institutional brand with greater clarity. This leads to identifying new action initiatives that will help achieve their goals. When this all happens they also come to realize that they must walk all this talk inside the institution in order to mobilize the troops to move the train. And the more people really know the fundamental subject matter (as opposed to just thinking they know it), the more effective the total institutional marketing initiative will become.

The ultimate outcome politically is that the people problems and the institutional barriers that surface in these discussions, the education that takes place and the team building that happens all go a long way toward creating the climate necessary for dealing with problems effectively.

ACTION TEAMS

Action teams are typically formed to implement new initiatives that need to happen over and above routine activities. But the same political advantages associated with the task force are built into this process, too. These teams comprise researchers, writers, designers, events professionals and project managers. They take the brand message and transform it into targeted and interactive action. The political differences and jealousies that often divide these people when isolated in their silos now disappear in the interaction of teamwork.

Getting a variety of people exposed to what such a team can achieve is an effective political activity. Sometimes achieving this is just a matter of reporting to cabinet meetings, departmental staff meetings and individual opinion leaders about what the team is doing, who is involved and how much impact the team is having. Actions speak louder than words, and participating in that action or just feeling connected to it speaks loudly as well.

Serving on the task force that oversees everything, or being a member of an action group that designs and carries out implementation, or just even being present in a staff meeting where all this is discussed brings people on board and makes them feel involved. This feeling of involvement gives people the sense of a daily connection to what goes out and the results that come back. And for those who feel connected, the need for quantitative, piece-by-piece proof of results fades away.[1]

The tangible results of more and better students, more money and enhanced reputation come from the synergistic impact of multiple interactive communication tactics, and therefore it's virtually impossible to separate each tactic for evaluation. Either the orchestrated effort of the total campaign is working or it's not. And those who participate, even indirectly, get a feeling in the dynamic of the moment of either success or failure. That feeling is ultimately confirmed—or not—in the final numbers.

In other words, getting people involved is the way they learn about your field. And when they do learn about it, they stop asking you for proof that it works, and the climate is there for dealing with the politics.

EDITORIAL PRIORITIES COMMITTEES

This kind of committee is unusual for most campuses, but the political advantages of having such a group become immediately obvious. Having this committee will help you explain how you select the stories that need to be told and why you waste valuable professional time when asked to write and send useless press releases.

Simply put, this committee selects stories to reinforce branding, or competitive advantage themes. But because this committee is a new idea for most campuses, it should be recommended by a university-wide task force or similar body. This important and effective tool for establishing widespread brand understanding is the best mechanism I know of for demonstrating that a policy of editorial freedom can be maintained and still combined with a more systematic approach to advancing the brand. It also provides still another opportunity to deal with the many marketing-related political issues that arise.

Editorial freedom is maintained because periodicals and publications editors remain free to cover the stories and report the news as their judgment dictates. But an editorial priorities committee meets regularly to also find the stories that best reinforce the brand message points. These then are turned into large features, which are also given some prominence in their positioning. If some stories contain controversial elements or implications, so be it. So long as all sides are represented fairly, true stories can be told without harming brand identity. And by telling these reputation-defining stories over and over again, the brand-clarifying message topics are made visible and the brand identity is established and reinforced.

I have seen this approach to advancing brand themes work over a long period. Its tactical power derives from the fact that the themes are repeated over and over again. Specific stories will change, but the themes do not. Those that are repeated will be told from different angles and will still provide variety. And those that are so good that they appear everywhere, from basic brochures to presidential speeches, become the basis of legends and traditions. The political value of editorial committees is that they determine editorial direction by a participatory process, leave ample room for editorial freedom and demonstrate how careful story selection helps advance the institution.

Many times, brand confusion in the marketplace is the result of a well-meant communication assumption: namely, that more communication is better and that the role of the communication office is to send out more "stuff." But experience teaches that more communication is not better and that just sending out more and more messages only contributes to communication clutter and brand confusion. The antidote to this assumption is in setting message theme priorities, applying the theme priorities to story selection, determining priority market segments and selecting the right media for each segment. And the more those selected media are interactive, the better.

GRASS-ROOTS POLITICAL TOOLS

Above we discussed how the basic group and organizational process tools of integrated marketing can also become internal political tools. In addition, external political tools can be used to handle internal situations.

You must begin by understanding that the key to success is your ability to employ the process tools discussed above to your own political advantage and then to be persistent in your work without becoming too pushy or aggressive. Accomplishing this will require a large measure of consistency and patience. When dealing with intense people and serious institutional barriers, it's possible on any given day to feel that everything is falling apart. It's commonplace in this line of work to head home at the end of the day screaming at the top of your lungs that you are getting nowhere fast. But when you learn how powerful group processes can be, you are able to exercise both persistence and patience on a daily basis. Then the day will come soon enough that you can look back on the last several months and say, "Wow, look how far we have come!" Sometimes you can't really see the progress you have made until you stop and look back.

This fundamental understanding of process will enable you to use it as a framework to systematically implement a grass-roots political plan. Such a plan involves various components.

Identifying and activating your supporters

When a university-wide task force is launched and an account executive approach to marketing schools and programs begins, your best supporters will usually self-identify fairly quickly. Many colleagues will have been waiting for this approach to happen for a long time, and when the word gets out that something like this is in the wind, they usually show up with bells on. The key is not to take their support for granted, as often is the temptation.

Don't make the common mistake of thinking that you can count on these folks and that your biggest task will be to convert your detractors. Nothing is further from the truth. The fact is, your most important task will be to thank your supporters, to inspire them to walk the talk and to give them a role to play in this process. Put your best supporters on your task force, use the best talent on action committees and commission them all to generate the buzz that it's a new day at this institution and that the train is about to leave the station.

Ignoring your detractors

Detractors of marketing and advancement in universities are usually those people who have a fundamental negative outlook on almost everything. They are always prepared to fortify themselves for a debate, and they will always dig in when confronted. So the more you try to persuade them, the more negative they become. And the more you push them for support, the more they actively work against you.

So the best approach you can take with detractors is to just ignore them. That usually neutralizes them, and they just become inactive and dormant. Usually they do not end up affecting the dynamic of the organization in either direction; and before they realize it, the train is moving away from the platform and they are left standing there, wondering what happened. Detractors ultimately become non-players, and in most institutions they usually move on to be a detractor again at another time or in another institution.

Educating the neutrals

Those who are neutral about marketing, advancement or other issues are usually in the process of trying to figure out what they think. When we work with them on a task force or action team or committee, or are just able to brief and interact with them in staff meetings, we are able to educate them about the basics of integrated marketing and advancement. They will very likely be eager learners, get excited about future possibilities and very happily help walk the advancement talk. The newly convinced are the ones who become the most excited about announcing to the whole world that it's a new day at their institution.

The neutrals are particularly important because when you can add them to your supporters, you are most likely to have a majority—and that means you are finally on your way. The newly activated are the most motivated to tell the story, and the younger believers among them will become the future of the organization. So they are more than worth a little extra time and attention.

The newly converted young neutrals are especially important in this age of social media. Our objective in marketing always has been to get people talking, spreading the word everywhere they go—creating buzz to achieve brand power and high visibility. And today, when we talk about using social media to start the buzz, we are really only using new tools to generate positive messages by word-of-mouth. When young neutrals become energized, they go directly to social media and the buzz begins. It doesn't matter if they use Facebook, YouTube, Twitter or whatever is the next big social media platform. What does matter is that people are now talking and the train is moving ahead.

Making deals

Sometimes a dean or a provost will just not want to act. In the cases when you have taken the time to build a relationship, it's always possible just to put aside all other logic and say, "I need your help on this." The strong implication (sometimes articulated as well as implied) is that you will be there for that dean or provost when he or she needs your help and support in the future. And of course you must deliver when the time comes, even if it hurts a bit.

In the long run, most of the little things you give up in deal-making don't matter much, especially in light of the greater achievement of moving the train ahead. Trust me: It really works that way. We all want every little thing to be just right, from every tiny publication to individual pieces of advertising. But at the end of the day, the little ugly flyers and the one-time, unnecessary ad will do very little harm, and the greater good is always served by moving the train down the tracks.

Using third-party advocates

Sometimes you are not the right person to make the needed deal. Fundraisers know from their research which donors need to be asked for a gift and for how much. They also usually know when they are not the right person to do the asking. And so they must request that a third-party advocate make the ask. It's the same with internal institutional politics.

When you need the support of provosts, presidents, trustees or even some deans, the best approach is to first ask yourself, "Whom should I ask to do the asking?" It saves time, relieves stress and actually provides a little gentle pressure on your third party to get more involved as well. In the final analysis, this kind of grass-roots political approach is the way things get done in institutions.

OTHER POLITICAL ISSUES

There is a whole range of what I would call miscellaneous political issues that you will run into in institutions. Here are the most critical ones.

The poison of polarization

The dynamics of politics these days seems to force leaders at every level to move to the extremes of their positions. This is true in Washington, and it is also often true in organizations. Person A takes a position on an issue, and when Person B objects, the progression of the ensuing exchange pushes each person to the extreme of his position. Then people take sides and the controversy begins. Avoiding this situation is extremely difficult, especially in a competitive environment.

Solving problems in a management situation requires careful facilitation by an experienced moderator or chair. First, the problem should be clarified. Second, the tendency to argue the extremes should be acknowledged. Third, the fact that solutions are almost always in the middle of the extremes should also be articulated. Only then can the problem-solving discussion begin.

During the discussion, the moderator and the participants brainstorm and list solutions, and then further list the strengths and weaknesses for each possible solution. After tallying and analyzing the pros and cons, the moderator and participants come to a conclusion. The process is not easy, and the facilitation must be strong. But it is possible to have lively problem-solving discussions and still reach a conclusion, if not a complete consensus. The chair must also reiterate that most solutions are hardly ever perfect, so aiming for a perfect solution cannot be the goal and realizing that adjustments afterward must be anticipated as part of the process.

Polarization is indeed organizational poison, and once it enters the system and becomes tolerated or even encouraged, the management team becomes virtually anesthetized. From that moment, decisions on most important issues get tabled. One only needs to look at the U.S. Congress to see the consequences.

Left- and right-brain negotiations

Some people think in numbers and others think in concepts. Number thinkers reduce most arguments to rational conclusions based on statistics, and concept thinkers have more gray-area ideas based on human experiences and preferences. The politics of this situation can be complicated.

When left- and right-brain people come together to solve a problem, the real issue becomes who gets to define the problem and facilitate the discussion. Usually, concept thinkers will not have much of a chance in a numbers-based argument, and vice versa. So if victory is your aim, it's important to host the meeting so you can define the parameters of the discussion.

It's helpful when one of the parties clarifies the different ways each group is likely to approach the situation. Then before the discussion begins, each group acknowledges respect for the other and a willingness to be flexible in the search for a solution. If the situation is handled with good cheer and respect, it's actually possible that both will agree in the end that a better solution was found when both quantitative and qualitative perspectives, as well as flexible attitudes, were involved.

A seat at the table

In order to get the institution moving forward with new initiatives, you need to have your interests represented in the right way, in the right places, at the right time. Having a seat at the table does not necessarily mean that you have to be physically there yourself, in the short term, though in the long run you may need to have this physical presence for the sake of your career. Early in your professional life, however, you need to think more about finding mentors and third-party supporters.

So your strategy early in your career should be to analyze who is on the president's cabinet, the board of trustees, the dean's council or any other decision-making body and to identify someone or several people there who can represent a solid understanding of integrated marketing (or other advancement disciplines) in their meetings. Each group will no doubt look different to you and have a different set of players, so your approach should be to find someone on each group you can meet with periodically to brief on your activities and needs. In many cases you may even need to activate your teaching mode to gradually bring them up to speed on your latest thinking about strategic and integrated marketing. (See chapter 6, "The Marketing and Communications Professional as Teacher.")

In the final analysis, your value to the organization, and your career success, will be greatly enhanced when you have these other leaders, both colleagues and volunteers, championing your cause in their meetings. It will feel frustrating to not be there in person, but it is a mistake to push hard to get there too soon. That looks self-serving and too much like empire building. Your physical seat at the table will come in time, at this university or somewhere else.

"A prophet in his own land"

One of the biggest frustrations for would-be organizational leaders is the way in which talented people moving up in their profession are often regarded by colleagues around them. The old adage that a person cannot be a prophet in his own land too often plays out to be true—at least for a while.

This situation can be attributed to many reasons. One is that people tend to see you in the same light as when they first met you. So when you start to move beyond their perception of who you are and what you do, those people have a hard time changing their view. Many become skeptical that you are just a climber and care more about yourself than about the institution, and they react to you accordingly.

Many more, however, are just plain jealous. They have a hard time feeling good about someone else's successes in a workplace where they, too, are trying to be successful. And so your successes are never acknowledged the way you expected, and you do not get the automatic cooperation that you feel you deserve. It just doesn't seem fair.

The best strategy in this situation is to just keep going. You cannot stop achieving because others are not responding to you the way you want. Their reaction is natural, and your situation is one you will need to get comfortable with. Obviously, you need to proceed carefully and thoughtfully, but the best approach is to keep moving ahead. Even though you are not getting credit for your efforts, you need to continue to give credit to others. You need to be the model of what you want for yourself. In the end, your recognition will come. It may actually come first from outside your institution. Many people who are celebrities in their fields remain unknown or unacknowledged within their own institution. This is a reality of professional life, and you will get used to it sooner or later.

As you proceed through your career, relationships change. As we have discussed before, some friends drop away because you do not have much in common any more, or they just can't see you in a new role. Others continue to admire you or are moving up with you. And, of course, you will make new friends and colleagues who are compatible with where you are, as well as where you are going. All of this is natural, but the pain is rarely anticipated and it can obscure the joy of making a difference, at least for a while. It just does not feel like you want it to, and it certainly is something you were not told about earlier on. The lesson is that your joy will come from looking back on how far you've come and not on feeling complete where you are.

Career insecurities

Everyone experiences feelings of insecurity. Most of us did not anticipate how often the situation would be repeated and for how many years. Every time a new boss appears, you will feel insecure for what seems like a prolonged period.

Every time a new president arrives, you will feel unsettled again. Every time a problem arrives in your area, you will feel your job could be on the line. And every time an employee gives you a hard time, you will feel concerned about how your reputation might suffer as a result.

Experience teaches (if you pay attention to it) that if you help lead the coming change you will be more secure than if you worry or show concern about doing things differently. And when you have some forward momentum established, a few glitches along the way will not matter at all. You may have that insecure feeling in your stomach from time to time, but if you can keep that train running down the track you are more than likely to be fine.

The problems arise when you pause too long or get wrapped up in a troublesome situation or start looking too concerned. Then your natural feeling of concern starts to look like insecurity and uncertainty, and you become vulnerable. When you show too much vulnerability, you lose that leadership aura that others admire and doubts about your leadership begin to creep in all around.

Looking confident and learning how to maintain that look, even when you are not feeling it, is the key to success. During times like when you're feeling a bit shaky, it's helpful to have a daily action plan. Step back each morning, list the issues you see coming that day and write down some action steps based on all you now know about politics. You will need to be sensitive and also look confident. Address problems head-on during times of change without looking insecure in the moment. And a daily plan is an important tool to use.

Relating to a new president

When a new president arrives, he or she is likely to quickly communicate that there is a lot to be done for this university to achieve its potential. This might sound to you as though the new president is saying that the previous administration did not do enough to put this place on the map, and thus you and your colleagues may immediately feel vulnerable. In fact, in some cases the new president may actually be signaling that other leadership changes will be coming.

This is a difficult situation, and it makes almost anyone who had responsibilities with the previous administration feel defensive. Your natural reaction will be to want to tell the president about all the wonderful things that were accomplished. Of course you are willing to say there is a lot left to be done, but you will really have strong feelings that past accomplishments should be acknowledged, even applauded, as a steppingstone for what is to come.

An experienced new president will usually acknowledge past accomplishments quickly. He or she will talk about standing on the shoulders of those who came before and will explain that a wonderful foundation has been laid for greatness yet to come. But even when this approach is taken, you are still likely to feel a bit of vulnerability. Your concern will remain that the new leader is probably thinking that a new team will be needed to establish a new day, and such an outcome would leave you without a job.

Indeed, when a new president arrives, losing your job is a possibility, and it's wise to have a plan in place for such an eventuality. But such an outcome is not always in the cards. It is true that most new presidents are looking for people who will become loyal new team members and bring fresh new ideas. But it's also true that they will need some people close at hand who have some past institutional knowledge about players and processes and who can help make a time of transition more effective. New presidents are concerned about their success too, and they are aware that a successful transition will depend on their savvy handling of politics as well.

A successful strategy for you just might be to approach the new president from a position of excitement about needed change. Your position might be to characterize what you have done so far as laying the groundwork for what is to come, but you could also acknowledge that you have come to see that new leadership right now is what the institution needs. So acknowledge that change is needed and say you are eager to help in any way you can.

Helping to lead change is always a more secure place to be than holding back and quietly thinking, "This is just not the way we do things here." When you find yourself thinking that, you can be sure you are sending those vibes to everyone around you. And this is when your job becomes insecure. But when you step up and convey that you have been waiting for new leadership and are ready for this new day, you very well could become the most valuable staff person the new president has in making this transition successful.

Surviving failures

It's almost a cliché to suggest that if you have had no failures you are not taking enough risks. But in the marketing world (and probably throughout advancement) that is clearly the case.

Throughout my career, I have tried to help others avoid the big mistakes I have made. But even though I can help you avoid some big mistakes, I think it is even more helpful to teach about the tools that will be needed to success-fully learn some of these lessons the hard way.

Risk is always involved when you try a new idea or launch a new initiative. You do your best to do the research and analyze the pros and cons; but in the final analysis, when you step out with something new it always can flop. And so just what can happen after a fiasco?

In retrospect, you'll find that many of the little things, and even a few of the big ones, you will worry about never really matter as much as you thought they would. This is especially true when the train is moving forward overall. One embarrassing publication, or an advertisement that doesn't work, rarely has the terrible consequences you fear. Most of the time, few people will even notice what seems horrifying to you. Those who do notice forget about it soon after they lodge their protest. If your marketing program is working, the negativity surrounding a mistake never lasts long, even when your president gets upset at something that went public.

Your biggest problem will be to overcome your disappointment in yourself and your own tendency to be paranoid about such things. Creative people are usually harder on themselves than others are on them. Often it takes a while to put setbacks aside and move on—but you will need to learn how to take them so much in stride that you move on to the next initiative before you think twice about it. By doing so, you continue to look like you know what you are doing, and that is the main factor in remaining secure in your job.

It's important to remember that you learn so much more by your mistakes than by your successes. I often find myself confessing to my students that I learned these lessons first by doing them all wrong. And while as their teacher I am working to eliminate unnecessary failure from their careers, a certain amount of it is healthy, and maybe even necessary, to prepare them for real institutional leadership.

Making others heroes

Making heroes of others is a lot of what the profession of marketing is all about. Much of what advances the institution is the major achievement of its people—whether the president, deans, star faculty or staff—and the public visibility and recognition that they get.

Bringing this recognition about is often more difficult than it seems. In some cases, these people are reluctant to step out, and in others they are not able to perform well under pressure. It is an often-experienced disappointment to discover that someone does not want the publicity she deserves or is unwilling to take the next step in her career that you could facilitate because that person is satisfied where she is.

The political challenge is to find people who will work with you and to spend your time mostly with them. As they become prominent in their field, you also must continue to work at becoming prominent in yours. And while many people might resent the recognition that you are getting in your profession, you will find that as you gain prominence in your field you also are enhancing your ability to enable opportunities for others.

After all, prominence these days in advancement means you also know people in other education associations and institutions, and these people know everyone else. In other words, with prominence in this field comes membership in a network of professional leaders who can help you and who can help you help others.

NOTES

1. Professionals in marketing, for example, often find themselves frantically grasping for adequate responses when someone higher up (or even lower down) asks them to prove what they are doing is working. They are often asked questions like: How do you know this ad is worth the money? That's a nice brochure, but how do we know it's producing results? These questions are almost impossible to answer definitively. But those involved in the process, both directly and indirectly, can just "feel" from their daily interactions with each other and the market whether or not it is working. This outcome alone makes the participatory approach worth all the time and effort.

CHAPTER 4

Situations You're Likely to Encounter

PROFESSIONALS in marketing, communications and other advancement areas are likely to encounter a vast number of situations that will require political savvy, and it's obviously impossible to identify and analyze them all. I have found, however, that if you think through a number of the scenarios that others have encountered, you will understand the kind of strategic thinking you will need to address all the other surprises. Political situations are like crises: Each one you face seems dramatically different from the others you have handled, but having worked through others gives you the basic process tools you need.

THE POLITICAL CHALLENGE OF ADVANCING ADVANCEMENT

Advancing advancement for marketing professionals today means helping development executives rethink the future of back-to-back campaigns and then designing initiatives to maintain donor loyalty when so many other organizations are competing aggressively for their support. It also means helping alumni relations executives see the incredible potential of the lifelong connection of their program to the entire institution and then designing initiatives to make that a reality. For marketing and communications to be able to help rethink the very foundation of these disciplines, it's important for executives to understand how far M&C has come.

Indeed, in the past 10 years the overall field of university advancement has moved from not even daring to utter the "M" word to now linking it to "communication." Together, they have become a separate advancement discipline. CASE, in fact, officially refers to the discipline as "communications and marketing." Both development and alumni relations are realizing that remaining competitive and advancing their disciplines will involve taking a hard look at implementing strategic marketing and communication.

Once again we point out the increasingly important teaching function of the marketing and communications professional, and approaching the situation with a great deal of savvy also applies here. I have found that if you approach your advancement colleagues by explaining what you are already doing in the new-media world, for example, you will find yourself involved with their strategic planning as a natural outcome of the conversation. If you conceive of the "teaching" part as a project over time, you will find that the end result is an ongoing planning process where you truly integrate all the advancement operations in a permanent way. And that's what you will really need to accomplish in order to help your institution face the new marketplace with confidence.

DEALING WITH THE "ACADEMIC" PRESIDENT

All types of university presidents, from corporate to scholarly, can be found on our campuses. One of the most interesting types these days is an academically trained and focused president who is trying to figure out how to face this competitive and rapidly changing marketplace.

I have worked with a number of these types of leaders in a number of different settings. They tend to see the need to be more aggressive, but they still want to believe deep down that the "build it and they will come" approach might work. They are willing to do some marketing, but not too much. One such leader would say to me, "OK, Lauer, we will do this, but we will not do that." I could have been frustrated by this leader, but over time I came to realize that I should be happy: I was getting support for half of what I thought we needed to do and I accepted that support cheerfully as I planned the next step. Moving such an academic-oriented leader ahead in increments became my key strategic approach. You will find that as your suggestions work without bringing too much angst to the administration you can actually begin to move the train ahead.

I have found that the academic president usually is financially conservative and finds it difficult to spend significant resources on marketing. She is not likely to change this financial perspective, but incremental improvement is better than none. And taking one step at a time is likely to be good enough to keep your institution in the game.

WORKING WITH A CORPORATE-THINKING PRESIDENT

Current trends seem to suggest that your next leader is likely to be a corporate thinker. I do not necessarily mean that this leader will come from business; rather, more people with academic backgrounds are acquiring administrative and budgeting experience earlier in their careers.

As you might imagine, a corporate-thinking president is the most supportive of a marketing orientation, which just means that all strategic planning is done by aligning institutional strengths with external marketing and social trends. This is often not the natural approach of the academically focused leader, who tends to see universities as a collection of traditional academic fields doing high-quality teaching and research. Marketing-oriented, corporate-thinking leaders are more likely to look for academic strengths that can give the institution a competitive advantage over the competition, and then build them so they link directly to meet current market needs.

This thinking clearly aligns with that of the professional marketer and communicator, and so the political strategy should be to find every way possible to cultivate a relationship of ongoing collaboration.

It's not unusual for the marketing person to have daily meetings with a corporate-thinking president. Touching base regularly establishes a setting and a sense of institutional timing that every marketing practitioner craves. And so you will want to develop a relationship-building mind-set and a tone that tactfully assumes regular collaboration. It's important to realize that the self-fulfilling prophecy can work for individuals when their communication tone subtly carries such assumptions. In fact, it's amazing how it can work, but only when leadership styles are compatible and the people involved see eye-to-eye on the fundamentals of moving the institution ahead.

ACCOUNTING FOR EGOS

It's safest to assume that every leader has a huge ego. In other words, you should assume that no one likes surprises and that everybody wants to feel looped in to every important transaction. You should also assume that all leaders want their accomplishments recognized and that it's always better to overhype them. Never assume their declared modesty is how they really feel. You should assume all leaders like to be in the company of prestigious VIPs, and so you should think up opportunities to create these situations.

The more you do these things, the more your interests will be supported. No doubt about it. Yes, many leaders will assure you that some or all of these efforts do not matter to them. But don't believe them. And even if they mean what they say, you will still be better off building them up than ignoring them at the wrong time. Trust me: Treat them like they all have big egos.

WORKING WITH A VISIONARY PRESIDENT

Visionaries can be exciting to be around. Assuming they are in the right place at the right time, that excitement can be contagious and mean all the difference to an institution.

A few important conditions must exist, however. First, the institution has to be ready to step out, because even a visionary can't do it alone. Second, visionaries have to know how to gather the right kind of teams around them because they usually have needs that go beyond normal management. They can be impatient, say things about what they want that are unrealistic at the moment and be ruthlessly demanding.

Visionary leaders also have the potential to be hazardous. They often shoot from the hip and can play favorites on their team, creating morale issues and a competitive environment in the executive suite. While having a visionary leader can be really exciting for a while, only time will tell if this leader's tenure will all come together or end abruptly with an urgent presidential departure.

Having a visionary leader at your institution can be a great time in your career—if the timing is right. By "right timing" I mean that the institution needs a visionary who can articulate new possibilities and you are ready for a wild ride. It's important to match your personal and professional needs, psychologically and professionally, with the person's expectations and quirks. What looks on the surface like a great opportunity can turn sour very quickly when the rocket ship takes off. These will be the very best of times or the very worst. But no matter, you will learn a lot, and that's the attitude you must have.

THE PROBLEM-SOLVER PRESIDENT

Sometimes the institution has a problem and a leader emerges who seems to instinctively understand it. That person either has a solution in mind or, better yet, understands how to design an effective process to find the solution. Such a person can appear to be a visionary because he understands this institution's unique situation, but he will turn out to be more of a systematic planner and leader and just might be even more rewarding to work with than the visionary. This president should represent another opportunity for a process-oriented integrated marketer.

Your strategy should be to first find out what strategies or processes the new president has in mind. Then you can relate what you know about process and planning, which has been discussed in previous chapters. Through conversations you will gradually begin to offer to help both collaborate on the design of the project and manage it. If your offers are accepted, bingo! you are part of the inner circle. As the president finds and begins to articulate solutions, you are there to add the visionary tone to the rhetoric.

I am thinking now of a school in Canada where part of the marketing problem was a decline in population in the province. The perfect person to lead the institution was already inside it, waiting for the opportunity. When that person was promoted into the position, a marketing person was hired with destination marketing experience. The combination seemed perfect, and the marketing program became an integrated model.

WORKING WITH A NUMBERS-ORIENTED PRESIDENT

Academic leaders who bring with them a numbers-based research background tend to have certain characteristics in common. They expect cases for change to be based on statistical analysis. They carefully prepare for conversations and meetings by going over the numbers, and they expect those who relate to them to do the same. Because they do their homework and expect everyone else to do their homework too, they tend to have an aura of strong self-confidence.

I have encountered many presidents like this. Let me reiterate that the challenge for the marketing person will be to determine whether you are a quantitative thinker or whether you are more of a creative strategic thinker. The quantitative marketer is likely to base most recommendations on numbers-based research and will be fine with this president. But the creative thinker, and there are many in the marketing field, will take data into account but base recommendations more on experience in the trenches and gray-area judgments about institutional momentum. I found this tendency to slight the numbers to be a real problem in working with numbers-oriented presidents, so let me address it a bit more.

The creative person will need to be armed with some numbers when meeting with the quantitative leader. If the numbers person has called the meeting and set the agenda, it's not the time to propose creative projects. Rather, your strategy should be to look at the numbers and to defer big decisions on actions. Another meeting should be called for which the creative person sets the agenda, with additional participants selected because they can help provide solid support for a creative action proposal. In the final analysis, both quantitative-based and creative-based ideas need to be considered. How this comes about will be determined by how the meeting of these minds takes place.

The creative marketer survives with quantitative leaders simply by affirming the value of numbers, demonstrating an ability to deal with them and becoming savvy enough to survive quantitative-based meetings by calling separate creative-based ones at another time. This not only can work, but it can work well. The best decisions always come from bringing all ways of thinking to the table at the outset, and then also having a process in place that enables gray-area solutions to emerge over time.

The worst-case scenario for the marketing professional is when the numbers-based president's confidence turns into arrogance, and his or her lack of appreciation for creative people turns to cynicism about them. I have seen some autocrats actually discourage talented people by treating them like they are too big for their britches. If this happens to you, I would suggest that looking for another team to work on is wise.

TRADITION-BOUND PRESIDENTS

Another presidential style mentioned before is the one in which the person takes the job to try to make the institution into an image of an ideal university. I have noticed this to be the case more often (but not exclusively) in large public institutions rather than in smaller privates.

Each institution has its own founding mission, its own management culture and is at a particular stage in its own historical development. And too often when a leader arrives on the scene with an image about what the ideal university should look like, the situation becomes problematic.

I cannot underscore enough the point that trying to make a university something it's not leads to a struggle between the natural inherent dynamics of the institution and the leader's autocratic insistence to develop it in a particular way. Such a struggle stops forward movement, and the university ends up on a plateau until a new leader arrives. True leadership studies the founding mission and inherent potential of each institution and develops that potential into differentiated excellence. And so if you find yourself working with this president you may be able to survive; but if you want to practice differentiated marketing, it is time to look for another job.

THE PRESIDENT'S CHIEF OF STAFF

A talented chief of staff can be very effective in helping keep an institution moving, so developing a strong relationship with such a person can be a great asset to the advancement professional. The position usually involves managing the president's office, handling schedules and shielding the president from unnecessary distractions. A strong relationship with the chief of staff can mean important help in keeping your efforts on the president's mind and in gaining access to the president when it's needed.

A serious problem can develop, however, when the chief of staff enjoys the power too much, behaves as the gatekeeper to any access to the president, becomes overprotective of the president's time and acts as an adviser to the president in areas where there is no real expertise. The problem becomes really serious when senior executives start sensing that the chief of staff assumes this is a higher position on the team than they have and that they no longer report directly to the president. The skillful chief of staff knows how to serve both the president's needs and respect the executive status of the other senior people.

I knew of a chief of staff who actually assumed advancement responsibilities he had not earned and should not have had. He planned the president's travel to set up donor contacts without consulting anyone in advancement. Thus, advancement had not prepared for the president's visit and wasn't in a position to follow up. And what's worse, decisions about donor calls were not made in collaboration with the previous work or planning by advancement staff.

In another situation, the president's chief of staff planned specific marketing or communication initiatives, such as events or publications, and then with the power of the president went directly to marketing and communications staff to tell them what to do. Again, the result was uncoordinated initiatives that just added to communication clutter and undermined the authority of marketing and communication leadership and the potential impact of a more integrated approach.

When the chief of staff position is not working well, it would be wise to consult with fellow senior executives and then meet, as a group, with the person. It's entirely possible she is completely unaware of how she is being seen, and you all can easily reach an agreement about how the president's office and schedule can be productively managed.

In the case of a chief of staff who ignores the problem, the senior people will have to bring the problem as a group directly to the president. When this becomes necessary, it's extremely important to come forward with a constructive proposal for a changed process rather than a direct attack on the president's chief. Most presidents will get defensive at first when confronted with the problem. Savvy is always called for in institutional politics.

In rare situations, it might be that the chief of staff relationship is only difficult for one of the senior people. If that is you, it is a bad sign, because that usually means the president has asked the chief of staff to deal with you more directly. If this is the case, the time has come for you to have a conversation with the president about how well things are going. It always works better for you to learn about dissatisfactions in a meeting you initiate.

GETTING BAD NEWS FROM A PRESIDENT

Your relationship with the chief of staff might be where you get the signal that you have problems with the president, or it may just be in vibes you pick up on in your working relationship or at regular meetings. It's always best to periodically have a "how am I doing" conversation. I now suggest that senior staff do that regularly.

If there are problems, you learn about them early on, when it's still possible to put in place a plan to resolve them. But if the situation is one that cannot be resolved and a separation becomes necessary, you can orchestrate a process that benefits you better in a meeting you call, rather than in one the president calls. You are in a much more positive position to negotiate the separation when you are leading the conversation. You are making it easier for the president, and it's likely to result in a better deal for you.

INABILITY TO MAKE DECISIONS

I have not seen this trait in too many presidents, but I have seen it in many other managers. It's a serious problem whether it manifests itself in the person you report to or in someone who reports to you. Whenever anyone says, "I will do it," and then doesn't, there is a serious problem. Likewise, when a person lacks the confidence to take a risk and hides behind doing more studies or just deferring with excuses, the train stops moving.

Let me share one example. The head of advancement at a particular institution had come into a very difficult situation. Several previous vice presidents had failed in this job, and the challenge was to find out why. Research and assessment studies were conducted, but as data came in, no action decisions were being made. One study would lead to more studies. Eventually, nobody on the staff could understand why the day had not yet come when studies were finished, analysis completed and a plan of action announced. And while this advancement leader truly believed more information was needed, no one else did. Neither the president of the institution nor the advancement staff could understand why they were not moving forward. Ultimately, the staff refused to follow this leader and the president decided to make a change.

An important trait for leadership in all areas of advancement is the ability to act and to launch new and exciting initiatives with confidence. A certain amount of study and collaboration should precede action, but it's also important to know when to start a new program, and many times this must happen before all the information is in. In the case of marketing and communications, we could argue that the information is never completely in, since today's new communications tools offer constant and immediate feedback. However, with any new program there is always an expectation for action in a reasonable about of time.

LEADERSHIP SPOUSES

In some institutions today the role of a presidential spouse is seen as a complicated and pressure-filled job, so performance expectations are spelled out in an agreement when the president is hired. It's important that everyone know what those expectations are. This is especially true for advancement people, because most of the time those expectations relate to external situations that will involve them. When everyone is clued in and gets along, problems rarely arise. But I have seen at least two impossible situations.

The first was a spouse who was very demanding of staff, particularly with the staff who served the president's home. Whether intended or not, the spouse was perceived as disrespectful of lower-paid and minority employees and demanded far too much of them for a university setting. Eventually the spouse's reputation as a difficult person became widespread inside the university and out, and it adversely affected the dynamics of many external situations. What made this situation impossible was the president's denial of it, and so it could not be constructively discussed. In the end, it contributed to a negative component in the long-term legacy of that presidency.

The best solution to a situation like this would have been to find a constructive way to bring it to the attention of the president and (best yet) the spouse as well. That approach would have involved careful third-party intervention and a great deal of savvy. In this case, however, those most closely involved had to accept that the president's denial was so complete that a constructive conversation was impossible. When you know that the situation is not likely to change, you just go forward as effectively as you can.

Another even more difficult situation involved a spouse who had previously been a public relations professional. She had strong opinions about the marketing and communications program of the institution and could not keep her views to herself. Many times she even got involved in the marketing and communication initiatives. Over time she became very critical of the marketing and communications staff, but denied that she was interfering. Her lack of confidence in M&C leadership became widely known as well. She said she was mostly concerned with events, invitations and materials directly related to the president's activities, but the widespread perception was that her dissatisfaction and involvement went way beyond that. Eventually the president asked a consultant to explain the situation to his wife. It's unclear if this situation improved, but the marketing and communication leadership did change.

WHEN STAKEHOLDERS WANT TO BE INVOLVED

This does not happen as often as feared, or at least this has been my experience. When these situations do arise, they can be resolved, especially where all the players get along and can work together. I always have taken the position that I will be happy to cultivate a relationship with anyone—spouse, trustee, faculty member, anyone—with marketing and communication expertise. I'm sure that I can impress them with what my staff knows about our industry, and we can always benefit from new ideas. I welcome their participation, which usually turns out to be rather limited in the end. It's very rare that such people actually want to direct decisions.

I worked with one trustee for a major public institution who was a retired marketing executive for a major bank. He definitely wanted to be involved. He was willing to acknowledge that higher education was an industry he did not know, and I acknowledged that I could learn a lot of marketing from his experience in banking. We had frequent conversations during which we exchanged ideas. In the final analysis, he was my biggest champion with other trustees, the president and even with members of the president's staff.

A POWERFUL CFO

When dealing with chief financial officers, it's important to understand their training and the incredible pressure of their responsibility. And it's also important to cultivate a good working relationship with them, no matter how difficult you may find them.

For those who study finance and accounting, the entire organization begins and ends with revenue and expenses. The budget is at the core of everything a CFO does, and being the ultimate manager of the budget gets a CFO into everyone else's business, with a large measure of control. Presidents and trustees become comfortable with this arrangement, especially if they trust the CFO to keep them out of trouble.

Some of the same qualities and attitudes that distinguish a CFO can also be true of people in marketing. To the marketing professional the entire organization can be seen as one giant marketing machine, and everything begins and ends with marketing. Knowing consumer needs and meeting them with the right products, services, price and communication is what the job is all about. So both CFO and chief marketing officers will see the entire organization from their own vantage points.

During tight financial periods the marketing professional will argue against making cuts to marketing and in favor of actually considering new marketing and communication initiatives. The CFO will expect M&C to consider trimming back like everyone else and will only accept another approach if he or she can see a clear, immediate return. To the CFO, spending more money during tight times is not wise. To the marketing professional, that is precisely the time to protect your institution's brand identity and secure its future.

The CFO is also likely to see pricing (e.g., tuition, fees) as coming under his office's oversight. The marketing professional, however, will see price as an exchange of values that involves much more than money and discounts. It involves an emotional relationship with the consumer and has a lot to do with perceived value.

The battle between these vantage points is a part of the political process of the work. Your relationship with the CFO, and the support you get, will be defined in large measure by the support you have from your executive colleagues. There truly is strength in numbers. If your colleagues are marketing-oriented and take pride in what they see you doing, you will get further at budget time. And your colleagues' support will largely depend on how much they see marketing activities actually benefiting them. So taking time to build mutually supportive relationships with your executive colleagues is critical to your success with the CFO.

It doesn't hurt to let the CFO know you understand the nature and pressure of the job. That will help you a lot. Even so, you still may find it difficult to resist the tendency to resent the CFO's seemingly pervasive power, apparent influence over the president, relationship to the most powerful trustees and salary. The whole thing may still seem out of balance. But an understanding of why finance is so often at the center of everything and how to build your strategic relationship with the CFO will save the day when you need the day saved.

THE STAFF "GETS IT" BUT THE ADMINISTRATION AND SOME FACULTY DO NOT

This problem is not as prevalent as it once was, but it still exists in many institutions. Some people in higher education still do not see how marketing can help them clarify what the institution is and do a better job of helping it be understood in all the right ways in all the necessary places.

I am thinking now about one institution that based its past preeminence on its strong cooperative learning program. Time in school alternating with time on the job was the hallmark of the program; and based on the top quality of that total experience, the school was seen as a national leader in technology education. Past prominence would secure its future—or a least that is how it seemed to administrative officials.

Staff members, however, saw the situation differently. They knew that other institutions—some of which were nearby—were gaining in technology education reputation. They also saw that the whole concept of cooperative education might be fading away and that this basic premise at least should be reexamined and possibly revitalized. To this end, they were interested in integrating program planning with marketing, and many also hoped these integrated collaborations would lead to a new strategic plan.

When the need is perceived mostly at the staff level, and within mostly one office, progress is possible but will take a long time. The professional with a strong personal commitment to the institution, as well as patience and persistence, is likely to have a good career here. The impatient professional, however, will need to look for an institution with a different set of players and conditions.

At another institution, a faculty union in negotiation for new salary contracts posed a difficult set of dynamics related to launching an integrated marketing program. Timing was the main issue in this example. Clarifying brand identity and launching a more focused and integrated marketing initiative seemed to be a way to address the economic situation, which eventually would improve faculty salaries. But it wasn't the right moment to convince the faculty that spending more on marketing now would benefit them later. So again patience and persistence was needed.

In this case, a rather comprehensive project was launched immediately to clarify the institution's brand, and special attention was given to involving faculty and their leaders in the deliberations. Also, students, staff, alumni, donors and even community leaders were included so the recommendations would be based on broad and comprehensive participation. A good measure of patience and persistence was indeed required, but over time the faculty did not block the project and progress was made.

THE ROLE OF THE M&C EXECUTIVE

Some in the academy still insist on seeing the marketing and communication professional as a flack and marketing only as publicity. I am thinking now of a professional association where everyone agrees they need more marketing but each person has a different expectation of what that will mean. Some want a staff person who takes orders for services. Some just want a press release when they ask for one. Most want to be able to order a brochure or a video. Only a few understand what marketing really brings and see a real need for it.

The ideal role for the marketing executive is as an officer on the president's cabinet, advising on reputation building, crisis and issues management and on orchestrating the total institution in order to clarify institutional brand and program sub-brands, coordinate marketing initiatives focused on target markets and provide multi-platform and new-media support for student recruiting, fundraising and reputation building. This is a conclusion based on seeing many marketing programs at many institutions all over the world.

ASSESSING YOUR CAREER POTENTIAL

It is not essential at a given moment in time to have everything organized just perfectly in your life. In fact, the whole adventure of your career will be an evolution. For M&C professionals, you first need to know the integrated marketing story. You then need to be able to organize institutional processes to orchestrate integrated marketing initiatives. Next, you need to learn the politics of gaining support for what you are doing in an academic setting. And finally, the part about being on the president's staff will eventually come.

So do you know people in high places who will support your ideas about marketing? If not, get to know them now. Can you put essential processes together to get the right people collaborating, no matter the executive to whom they or their unit reports? If not, learn how. If you have these conditions covered, you have a major starting point. Get the train moving and see where it goes.

For me, the position of vice chancellor for marketing and communication and a partial restructure of the organization came only after I had a task force functioning, action teams performing, other committees working and lots of individual collaborations with the chancellor, deans, faculty leaders and others. If you do all this and that top job does not come for you where you are, I promise that it will be there for you somewhere else.

The future of higher education will be too competitive to think otherwise. Universities all across the globe are in the process now of putting advancement front and center in their administrations, and the executives the institutions will require will have to come from somewhere. Right now there are not nearly enough of you out there to meet that coming need. Stay the course, and you will help complete the invention of a whole new international professional field. Doesn't that sound like fun?

CHAPTER 5

Advancement in an International Sea Change

ENGAGING IN INTERNATIONAL EDUCATION is one thing, but understanding the implications of our industry becoming a total international marketplace is something else again. I have found that it is entirely possible for university administrators to be completely immersed in study abroad, faculty and student exchanges and even establishing campuses in other countries and still not be fully aware of how the international flow of students and money is undergoing dramatic change. For administrators to fully understand this change, the marketing officer may have to educate them. And the politics of doing so may not be easy.

Day-to-day student recruiting and fundraising can lead university leadership to see the future in terms of maintaining current markets, which are usually local and regional. Current positive and satisfying communication with prospective students and donors can be leading presidents and other officers to feel that this situation will continue.

But my travels in many parts of the world over the past 10 years or so have made me aware of just how quickly higher education is becoming international. The impact of initiatives taking place throughout North America, in parts of Latin America, the United Kingdom, Europe, Africa, the Middle East, Asia and Australia will soon be so pervasive that even the smallest institutions, which may not now consider their markets to be regional and do not aspire to market for students and money internationally, will be affected. Not only are institutions going to other countries to expand their influence; now, foreign institutions are or will soon be coming into your home market for their students and money, no matter where that market is. This assault on your home territory will be a game changer for the entire industry in all parts of the world, even if a particular institution considers itself to be only regional.

In *The World Is Flat*, Tom Friedman made us aware of how anyone, anywhere in the world with the right technology has an even playing field for becoming globally competitive. This is true within higher education as well. Hundreds of institutions from many parts of the globe are developing programs, exchanging students and faculty, raising money and visibility and recruiting students in all parts of the world.

Many administrations and faculty, however, still function as though the world has not changed. While they recognize some of the change in an intellectual, theoretical way, they are not really planning for it or understanding its implications for them and their institutions. The topic of internationalization of higher education comes up from time to time in meetings or in conversations with colleagues who travel, but too many leaders in too many institutions are missing the point of how rapidly change is happening and the extent to which it will significantly alter what we do in the future.

What must we teach institutional leaders?

GOVERNMENT ROLES ARE CHANGING

Almost everywhere in the world governments are changing the level or the nature of their resource support for higher education—or sometimes both. The trend simply is toward less and less overall support.

Governments around the world are facing numerous military, social and economic crises. At the same time, government leaders have developed the belief that universities today are in a better position than in the past to find their own sources of revenue. From tuition, to fees, to philanthropy from private sources, universities seem better able than other social enterprises to go it alone—or so these governmental leaders think.

In many cases the governments and societies that in the past viewed education as an entitlement for their citizens are beginning to consider the possibility that students and families should pay at least part of the bill in a cost-sharing formula. In the United Kingdom, for example, the change began with the addition of a modest fee paid by students, which for a while was the same fee no matter the school attended. Gradually, however, that fee increased, and it appears that the system is on its way to becoming more of a free-market enterprise, much like that in the United States. This same pattern can be seen developing in many parts of the world.

In the United States, access to higher education is a hot topic, and so financial aid to enable discounting the cost for those with financial need is a top priority. But at the state level, financial support for institutions varies significantly, depending on the condition of the state budget. Support for higher education in most U.S. states appears to be in a fairly steady decline. In some states that support is as low as 8 percent of a public institution's budget.

Institutional leaders need to be aware of changes not only in the level of governmental support but also in the types of programs being funded—and what this means for higher education. When governments support major investments in technology and engineering at colleges and universities, for example, criticism often arises, especially from academics, that the liberal arts foundation subjects are being neglected. So institutions are forced to consider on their own how they will fund research in vital subject areas such as history, philosophy, literature and music.

In some places, governments seem to be focused on career education and meeting the anticipated needs of the job market. When I visited several institutions in Australia, I heard concerns that this focus would lead to the neglect of the foundation subjects and that salaries were not competitive enough to attract talented faculty in these areas. Some also lamented that young people are expected to know what career they want to commit to before they even enter a university.

For many, this focus on job training significantly decreases the potential of higher education to be an enriching and life-changing experience. The question ahead then seems to be: Can success in philanthropy and increased student tuition and fees in institutions all over the world underwrite the total international enterprise in order to maintain quality?

PUBLICS ARE BECOMING MORE PRIVATE AND VICE VERSA

The United States has what is referred to as a dual system of higher education: One system is supported publically, the other supported privately. The public system generally has lower tuition, is very accessible and is heavily accountable to the public taxpayer. The private system is generally priced a bit higher, is more flexible in shaping educational and campus experiences and is mostly free of government control. But financial pressures from every direction are changing this picture. And what used to be a dual system may be in the process of becoming one system.

These days public universities are aggressively engaged in private fund-raising, and most of them have been quite successful. They are graduating thousands of students every year and are working hard to remind each one that neither their tuition nor their taxes paid the entire cost of their education. Publics offer naming opportunities for programs and buildings and give very public recognition to their donors. The more money they raise the more money they want, thus raising the fundraising goal with each and every effort.

Tuition is also going higher and higher in the public sector. While there is still pressure for publics to remain as accessible to the public as possible, government cutbacks in funding have resulted in pressure to allow tuition increases. And so over time publics are becoming more private. Some public institutions, such as the University of Virginia, began to talk some time ago about becoming private. Many more are also likely to consider this option in the future.

And while publics become more private, privates are also increasingly seeking public support. They want more financial aid support for students and more research support for faculty.

A desire to be more accessible to diverse communities adds credibility to the need for more publically supported financial aid. This is true both at the federal and state level. At the federal level, financial aid can help private institutions meet the society's objective to make a more diverse set of institutions accessible to those with financial need. (This diversity in types and sizes of institutions may be the most significant competitive advantage the United States has in the international market.) At the state level, private universities make the case that the state is actually saving money by offering financial aid to students who want to select a private institution. For example, when a state gives a stipend of $3,000 to a student to attend a private college, and that institution can complete a financial aid package necessary to enroll the student, and if it costs the state $6,000 for each student enrolled in a public institution, the state will save $3,000 for each student attending a private institution. These savings accumulate quickly. Available spaces are filled in private colleges, and the state reduces space needs in the public universities.

Private universities also seek funding for research projects, and private support only goes so far. Some major private institutions have received huge amounts of federal support; but with such large amounts of federal money coming to private schools, the old idea of "no government control" has gone out the window. When institutions accept such funding, they also accept the requirement to abide by regulations. And so the private nature of private institutions changes more and more every year.

With the re-passing of the higher education act in the United States, both public and private institutions will be required to report everything from crime statistics to loan practices and will be disclosing everything from student disciplinary processes to textbook prices to crisis alert communications procedures. So the distinctions between private and public institutions continue to blur.

All of this raises the question of whether or not the United States can maintain the advantage of institution diversity in type and size for the long term. Nowhere else can one select in one place from conservative church-related institutions to more liberal church-related ones, from medium-sized largely undergraduate colleges to very small liberal arts colleges, from huge public research institutions to large research-oriented private universities, from a general-education focus to career preparation in professional schools, from profit-making online enterprises to two-year community colleges.

Marketing practice encourages this kind of differentiation to enable building brand and establish competitive advantage. But are other forces also in place that are making institutions alike while marketing wants them to differentiate? Only a learning institution will be able to sort all this out to make the choices necessary to remain competitive into the future.

FUNDRAISING IS ALSO INTERNATIONAL

As institutions have graduated more and more people, and more and more of them are living in all corners of the world, it has been natural for fundraisers to follow these alumni, wherever they go, for annual giving and special project efforts.

Now, however, major gift officers are seeing opportunities for major project corporate, foundation and individual funding in many places, especially where institutions are opening campuses in other countries or forming substantial partnerships. Development programs are opening fundraising offices around the world and viewing fundraising market potential in much more global terms.

For example, universities in Europe have hired seasoned fundraising executives in North America to head their programs. Oxford University employed a successful fundraiser from the University of Toronto for a while, and the University of Edinburgh hired the former head of development at the University of New Hampshire. Their primary objective was to raise more money in North America for European universities, but by opening offices in other cities, they could intensify solicitation all over the world. Asian universities are also aggressively raising money in the United States, and Canadian institutions are expanding their efforts around the world as well.

Indeed, fundraising is a global enterprise and is becoming more and more competitive all the time. Every major nonprofit is asking how far it can expand its marketing and fundraising. From ballets to operas to symphonies, and from social welfare to aid organizations, the fundraising beat is heard far and wide. International NGOs and relief organizations are doing the same thing. And as universities establish themselves internationally, any respect for the idea that "these are your donors, not mine" is quickly going away. Every donor is being solicited from every direction, locally as well as internationally. And the appeals are the same: high personal or family or organizational recognition; a name on a facility or program; and, in more and more cases, a meaningful ongoing connection to the institution.

STUDENT RECRUITING IS MORE AND MORE INTERNATIONAL

A number of forces are converging to change the international student market. The situation has been evolving over a number of years, but the pace of change is now increasing rapidly as institutions modify their world view.

For some time, the United States has been recruiting students abroad, especially graduate students, partly because of the opportunities that these institutions present to bright students from all over the world for successful careers and lives. Another reason for this recruitment effort has been that foreign governments helped fund many of those students in the hopes of bringing the talent back home later. But these dynamics are changing.

As universities all around this "flat world" are planning their futures, many of them are working harder to keep their bright students at home. This is certainly true in parts of Asia, the Middle East and India. In the Middle East, aggressive efforts to attract select U.S. universities to open campuses there are seen as a way to bring an acknowledged superior U.S. education to their students on their own turf. It will be important for all of us to fully understand that university administrators in all parts of the world are now defining their futures in terms of their own self-interest, and they are making changes in order to become more internationally competitive.

These same administrators will be recruiting American students—graduates as well as undergraduates—to come to their universities in their countries. This certainly is true in Canada, although many U.S. students these days are having a hard time meeting Canadian entrance requirements. Universities in the United Kingdom are also looking abroad for more students, the result of rethinking how to fund the whole educational enterprise. Both U.K. and Canadian universities have added matched-funding incentives to raise more money at home and elsewhere. As price increases become more possible and more flexible, these institutions are motivated to think more competitively about where their students come from. And if the economy is moving now more toward European markets, and certainly more toward Asia, there is a compelling case to be made for U.S undergraduates to consider moving closer to the action to get an education that will prepare them to better compete in a world job market.

And what's more, many European and Asian universities are now offering many degree programs in English, especially in professional and business schools. The Indian Business School, for example, is stepping out to challenge the London Business School, INSEAD in France, Harvard, and other top schools. Universities in Europe are offering Asia-savvy education in English (as have universities in Australia and New Zealand for some time).

Most high school students in the United States are still too isolated to see the benefits of considering going abroad to college, but that will change as universities from all over the world come here more and more every year to recruit them. These students will find that, after the price of a plane ticket, the rest of their education might be as affordable as in the United States, or even more so. And there is little doubt in my mind that as Americans are more exposed to the rest of the world as study-abroad undergraduates, more and more will look abroad for schools offering programs in English for their graduate education.

And so educational programs, institutional partnerships, fundraising and student recruiting are all becoming international. As these forces take over our industry, the need for international visibility develops, too. Conveniently, the "flat world" provides new options for achieving this goal as well: As partnerships, agreements, study opportunities and programs emerge, the Internet knits the markets together and as social media follows and connects everyone, word-of-mouth and the buzz take over. Opportunities show up on YouTube and Facebook and are referenced on Twitter. And before you know it, your institution has gone global, often at very little cost, or none at all—except for the time it takes to put your message out there.

ADVANCEMENT PROFESSIONS MOVE FRONT AND CENTER

It's now easy to see why all the advancement professions are coming front and center in institutions all over the world. As governments cut back funding and change their role in regard to higher education and the marketplace becomes more competitive and international, advancement professionals are the ones who can save the financial day.

Money has to be raised, students recruited, visibility in the right places achieved, and appropriate programs developed. The good news is that we are more important than ever, are more likely than ever to be influential members of the executive team and be much better paid. But the bad news is that the job will be complicated, very time-consuming and full of pressure and certainly a lot more sophisticated.

Not only will we have to be teaching the institution more about what we do as advancement professionals, but we will also have to be getting better and better at what we do and inventing new tools to do our jobs. Communications technology and new-media practice are still evolving, research techniques are changing fast, fundraising practices will have to deal with the more-complex loyalty issue, the student recruiting marketplace is changing quickly and alumni relations will virtually have to reinvent itself. And while all this is taking place, you will have to teach others around you about it all, and politically achieve the support you will need to make it all happen.

Better learn to love the politics!

PART II

LESSONS FROM MARKETING AND COMMUNICATIONS

⇒◄ CHAPTER 6 ►⇐

The Marketing and Communications Professional as Teacher

FOR AS LONG AS I CAN REMEMBER I have found myself living simultaneously in at least three worlds: those of a thinker, a teacher and a practitioner. I was always thinking about everything and trying to put together in my head how the world works. Then I would sort out my thoughts by talking … and eventually by talking and teaching. Soon I felt the need to do something with all those thoughts, and eventually I realized that political strategy would be needed to get support for making it happen in an organization.

For a while in my teens, with the world changing around me, I thought the highest calling in life was to be a rock-and-roll DJ. I soon got that out of my system, but what stayed with me was the incredible potential of using communication as an instrument of change. And so as I made my way through college I found myself studying the social sciences, then international relations, and then philosophy, but all the time I remained interested in producing media. As a graduate student I found the field of public (noncommercial) radio and television, and that practitioner part of me has remained intact ever since.

In those days no one knew how to raise money in public radio, and so I moved into teaching. First it was to put bread on the table, but I became passionate about teaching when I discovered it was a way to talk about what I was thinking. I quickly found that I benefitted significantly from trying to explain as a teacher what I was learning as I was trying to actually do it—both my successes and my failures. And in time I found that writing what I was learning as a teacher and a doer was also important, as were the "political" strategy and tactics that I would need to make it all work.

And so the combination of thinker, teacher, doer, writer and political strategist sums up my journey. Political strategist came gradually at first by instinct, and then through lessons learned.

LESSONS LEARNED

My early days in radio were at WAMU FM in the 1960s, the public radio (then called "educational" radio) station in Washington, D.C.—which was and still is affiliated with American University, where I did both undergraduate and graduate work. I worked with Susan Stamberg, who eventually hosted NPR's *All Things Considered* for many years. She taught me a lot about what it took to produce programs that people would listen to, how hard it was to stay creative over time and just what would and would not work on radio. These were hard lessons to learn.

Eventually I found my way to TCU as a "baby" professor and continued my "practitioner" instincts in local television. At the time, broadcast stations were required by the FCC to donate public-service time, and so for many years I both produced and hosted programs, some of which set standards for low ratings. I learned the hard way that television was emotional and that it did not like a lot of detailed information. I learned that even the news programs would have to be lean in information and high in emotional intensity in order to draw viewers. And what I learned informed my teaching, and eventually my writing, as I tried to demonstrate how television changed the way everything worked, from your family life, to the way your children spend their time, to politics, to the way many would now come to worship, and to how people would learn (or feel) about the world. Much to my dismay at the time, I had to solve organizational political barriers and issues in order to produce any of these programs. Producing them was the easy part; getting to do it at all was the challenge.

During this time, I still enjoyed teaching—so much, in fact, that I told many of my colleagues that I would never consider going into administration. I was the typical young professor criticizing the administration, but I was still inherently the thinker, teacher and doer. After all, if I wanted to go into administration I would just go into business, where I could at least make some money. But my inherent make-up would change all that. One day the world turned on me. And politics were certainly involved.

As a young faculty member, I had been feeling that TCU was not keeping up in the rapidly developing world of adult continuing education and the creative approaches being used in other institutions. This was before community colleges had become the educational force they are now, and TCU was operating an evening college and noncredit program for adult students attending part-time.

Of course, I was outspoken in my criticisms in committee meetings and private conversations. So one day I was visited by an innovative young associate vice chancellor for academic affairs, who surprised me with a challenge: "Make something happen, Lauer, or keep your mouth shut." And so I walked right into the politics again and found myself realizing, in the process, that this was going to be the next practitioner role I would play, and think about, and teach about, and eventually write about.

And the politics now became a reality big time.

I had hard lessons to learn, and almost all would be about the politics of getting support to do things. My budget was inadequate for what I wanted to do. My administrative assistant (the only person who really knew what was going on in the office) quit abruptly. And I suddenly realized what an enormous job I had taken on: simultaneously designing new programs, teaching an entire institution focused on traditional full-time students about adult education, finding support for new and risky ventures and recruiting and inspiring part-time faculty and paying them virtually nothing.

During this period I added "marketing" to my communication portfolio, and I did it out of absolute necessity. It was no longer enough to communicate more effectively about what we were doing; now we had to design "educational products" that a specific market would respond to, set prices and discounts to be competitive and distribute those products at times and in places that would work for the market. It also meant more than promoting those products; we had to understand changes in media that were now moving beyond television. And it meant learning to love the politics enough to practice them every day. During those years, as I related to other nonprofits, agencies and organizations in the community, I found myself talking and teaching about both marketing and communication. Eventually I would be writing about them together as well.

But then the market changed and I had to learn another hard lesson. The community college system emerged and a number of new campuses were now opening. By now I had helped grow a major program at a nearby Air Force base, had met a need to enable workers at a local defense contractor to complete their degrees, had redesigned the entire summer school so it worked more like a third semester and had even brought limited college credit for life experience as an option for the highly experienced adult. But I started to see not only that the community college campuses would meet most of these needs, but that these changes would actually provide a wonderful opportunity for TCU to fine-tune its mission and better differentiate what it really wanted to become.

I therefore moved into external relations temporarily—or so I thought. A new chancellor had arrived, one who had been a dean at TCU and had returned to give birth to a new day. My thought was to help him get started and then move on. Who would have thought that the next 20 years would go by so quickly?

During those years I found that the marketing tools helped me think about how to position TCU as a major, medium-sized, doctoral-granting, private university with grand ambitions. Trying to introduce those marketing tools into a traditional environment was the start of the arduous process of bringing traditional academics around to support a more aggressive marketing effort. It was not easy, and it took many of those years. Indeed, I learned more hard lessons, and the politics I had learned in academic administration, combined with empathy for what academic deans and program heads deal with, came to bear now on how to get the academy to accept this new "M" word that would ruffle so many academic feathers.

During these years I wrote a book for nonprofit executives about using communication tools to advance their organizations. When I had the opportunity to write the book, I went to the chancellor, thinking that he might give me some time off to do it. Instead he said, "Don't think I will lower my expectations for your administrative work. But if I were you, I would find some way to do it." In other words, take it out of your hide if you have to, but do it.

Most years I also continued to teach, but now my communications interests had moved from teaching media studies to teaching about how organizations can communicate more effectively, and from the subject of communication to the combination of marketing and communication. My organization interests were moving from the larger nonprofit world to my own industry of higher education. As I evolved, my political awareness did too.

This evolution in both my practitioner and academic interests was necessitated by the growing realization that higher education was becoming more competitive every year and that TCU was not very sophisticated in how it was addressing the problem. Actually, at that time no institution was. But we had the experience and the staff at TCU now to figure it out—and so that is what we set out to do. Achieving this goal took long sessions with the staff and even longer sessions with the deans and others in the institution, always with mixed success. The result finally was a book about marketing higher education, and it turned out to be one of the earliest in the field. In that book I touched on the politics of making it happen, but just touched on it.

The program evolved now through two more chancellors, and so has the division of marketing and communication. I went from being director of university relations at the beginning of this professional odyssey, to an associate vice chancellor reporting to a vice chancellor of advancement, and then finally to vice chancellor for marketing and communication. But I also came to believe that most any organizational structure can work, if marketing is integrated into the thinking of everyone and if the processes are in place to enable the right people to work together.

MARKETING AS A WAY OF THINKING

The first political challenge is to get academics on board, and one of the most important lessons I learned along the way with academics was to always begin a talk with the idea that marketing is a way of thinking, not commercializing. First and foremost, marketing is a way to help institutions plan for and adapt to social change. It does not mean "just give them what they want." Rather, it means knowing how to connect with your audience's perceived needs, but then also knowing how to take them into new academic adventures and show them a world they never knew was out there. Thus, teaching the organization about what academic marketing really is about is the precursor to gaining support for doing it. Political strategy for winning that support must begin with education.

CREATING A LEARNING ORGANIZATION

I have been very influenced by the work of Peter Senge and his 1990 classic *The Fifth Discipline: The Art and Practice of the Learning Organization*. Senge argues that the only way to remain a leader in one's industry is to learn faster than the competition. This is true for organizations, and for advancement operations, too. Senge talks about an organization's having to overcome its learning disabilities. How true this is when it comes to marketing. There are so many misunderstandings and personal biases that need to be overcome to bring everyone to a common understanding of what marketing and communications professionals are really talking about. Learning how to learn together as a way of moving the organization forward is the prerequisite to real progress. And I have concluded that this educator role is one that the marketing and communications executive must accept if effective marketing is to get done at all. It's about imagining how team learning can occur in order to develop an organizational competence, which is what enables true leadership at both the unit and the institutional level. Articulate leadership is essential to organizational success, and the marketing executive must become one of those leaders.

The fifth discipline, the one that Senge references in his book's title, is "systems thinking." This kind of thinking is translating the great ideas generated into systematic, team-led, and doable action. It connects social trends with institutional strengths and puts ideas together to select the right actions at the right time. It is putting politics into action.

ESTABLISHING A COMMON UNDERSTANDING

Creating a common-ground understanding of marketing and communications in today's competitive market must be a primary objective of the learning organization, and thus it is the biggest challenge ahead for the future professional in the field. We need to learn how to form and launch the task forces, teams and tutoring necessary to out-learn the competition and then how to orchestrate the players into moving forward together. This in turn requires that you develop yourself as team leader and teacher and that you help enable that leadership in other units, as well as at the top.

CHAPTER 7

What "They" Should Know About What "We" Do

MARKETING AS A WAY OF THINKING is influencing change in all the disciplines of advancement. Thus, it is becoming more important every day that academic and other leaders learn more about the basic concepts of integrated marketing that are critical to advancing their programs and institutions, and every advancement professional needs to take on the challenge of delivering that message.

If achieving support for marketing requires teaching many people in the institution about the subject, the place to begin is with your own staff. Certainly everyone there needs to know what you are doing, have a same understanding of the subject matter that you do and be willing to walk the talk and share in the teaching.

Early on in my career I thought it was enough to go over the basics of marketing at annual staff retreats. But occasional remarks from my staff made me realize that some of them still did not get it and that we needed to spend more time learning the concepts.

I was appalled at how often even my close staff and supporters would arrive at a decision that made no sense in light of our brand standards, or at least in light of what I was assuming was our common understanding of what we were doing. And so in time, I understood that education and re-education about marketing basics would need to be a continuing part of frequent meetings with our staff as well as with every other group related to marketing the institution. Peter Senge was right: The organization that out-learned its competition would win. But the education would have to be continuous and become a part of the integrated process.

Later, as I learned how effective university-wide task forces could be, I realized that after my own staff, educating this group was the next step. The members of the task force will then help you walk the talk over time, and many of them will actually be able to help you teach others. You can also use them to brief other staff meetings in the institution and to accompany you to one-on-one branding clarifying sessions. The teaching begins with this group and ripples through the organization over time. We will discuss more about using task forces later.

Of course, getting literally everyone in the organization on the same page will never happen. But it is possible eventually to engage and reach a critical mass. Gradually, the train will start moving and, in time, pick up momentum. Finally, you'll discover that enough key people are on board to make the difference.

So if educating everyone is so important, we have to ask a number of questions: (1) What do we want everyone we can reach in the organization to know? (2) How do we decide how much information is enough? (3) How should we organize our "lesson plans"? (4) How should we deliver the goods?

During brainstorming sessions with several groups about how to answer the first question, I came up with no less than 22 items. And when I asked the brainstormers to talk about questions 2 and 3, their conclusion was to let each person determine how best to organize and present the 22 items. Some might want to just prioritize the items and concentrate on the most critical ones; others might prefer to cluster them in ways to reflect their priority problems. And for question 4, the thoughts generally were to go first to your staff, then to a university-wide task force, then to any meeting for which the staff is willing to put you on the agenda, and finally to use your one-on-one meetings with deans and department heads as both business planning and teaching moments.

Here are the 22 essential items that make up the integrated marketing subject matter, as determined from group discussions and institutional assessments in universities both public and private, as well as other associations.

1. THE MAIN PRODUCT IS THE "BRAND"

When translating the marketing subject matter to the academy, it is always helpful to return to the Four P's from Marketing 101: product, price, place and promotion. The fundamental questions here are: What is the product that we sell? Is it academic programs? Or is it the institution itself?

In the final analysis, the most enduring product is a person's lifetime identification with the institution. The quality and reputation of the academic program is important, but I believe that prospective students and parents think the academic programs are high quality at all institutions they are considering. Students and parents choose an institution because it is where they think they will fit in and they want to identify with it for the rest of their lives.

Thus, the importance of developing the brand identity and communicating it consistently is something everyone needs to understand and appreciate. It is critically important to the future success of institutions, and it is especially so in a changing and highly competitive industry. So education goal No. 1 in your institution is to get everyone to understand the importance of brand identity and to participate in developing and communicating it.

2. AN ACADEMIC BRAND IS A COLLECTION OF BENEFITS

An easy way to clarify an institutional brand identity is to form small groups of opinion leaders representing the major constituent groups of the institution and invite them to brainstorm the basic strengths of the institution. A facilitator then leads each group to reduce the list to the four or five features or benefits that best convey the competitive advantage of the institution. Your competitive advantage is defined by those features or institutional characteristics that differentiate the institution from its competition and position it so it can be presented as the best there is at what it does and whom it serves. These factors can be in several different categories, depending on the historical and developmental circumstance of the institution:

- Academic strengths (lead programs, liberal arts, technology)
- Values (community, personal development, ethics)
- Location (the coast, mountains, urban, rural)
- Lifestyle (elite, causal, artistic, studious, trendy)
- Campus look (modern, traditional, architectural features, color or tone)

Once the features or themes are identified, they will come together in words and phrases and convey a unified "feeling" or vicarious experience of the character or values of the place—in other words, its brand. From these phrases come lead sentences to use in copy, key words to repeat over and over and a tag line that when repeated consistently will carry the brand feeling forward. These words are important because they become a promise that a consistent experience will occur when on campus or when participating in the educational experience and that this consistency is a permanent feature of this institution. Achieving a widespread understanding of the power of brand is critical to marketing success, and so it's basic to the politics of gaining support.

The more people who participate in these brand-defining groups, the easier it will be to deliver the consistent "customer service" necessary to make good on the promise. This does not mean students should be seen as only "customers"; rather, it means they will expect as students to experience the brand.

Part of the branding process is studying the competition, i.e., benchmarking what they are doing that works. But be certain everyone understands that benchmarking should never lead to becoming like your competition; instead, it should help in differentiating you from them and in searching for the "blue ocean" that will allow you to sail right past them. One of my favorite books on this topic is *Blue Ocean Strategy; How to Create Uncontested Market Space and Make the Competition Irrelevant,* by W. Chan Kim and Renée Mauborgne.

3. EDITORIAL PRIORITIES REINFORCE THE BRAND OVER TIME

Magazine, periodical, and e-mail editors treasure editorial freedom, as do I. But I have come to see that within an organization it's possible for editors to have a great deal of freedom and still follow some very limited branding guidelines.

For example, one practice that works well is to form an editorial priorities committee, which takes the brand themes and searches for the stories in the institution that reinforce those points. There is a great deal of freedom within this approach to find specific "best" stories. The process does not prohibit the editor from also reporting the controversial news in addition to these stories. The news is the news, and the feature stories are selected to advance the brand. By maximizing the stories that advance the brand, printed publications and other media end up clarifying and advancing core strengths of the institution. And by having such a priorities committee you also have an effective mechanism for eliminating the trivial, less important stories that people want promoted even though they do little or nothing to advance the cause.

It's important to remember that in today's media-saturated environment, more information is not necessarily better. In most cases, an institution that floods the world with information will only end up contributing to information clutter and will not bring people to understand the real value of the organization. Communication is more effective when the overall message is narrowed and focused on specific market targets. And so the freedom to select the stories, but the willingness to use a committee to use branding points as a framework, can be one of your most potent and effective integrated marketing tools.

4. PRICE IS THE MOST COMPLEX STORY WE HAVE TO TELL

Marketing 101 explains that "price" means exchange of values. More specifically, price is the sum total of what a purchaser has to give up in exchange for what he or she gets in return. Price, therefore, is not just what a person pays in money, and what a person gets might be more than just the immediate service or product. This is fairly easy to understand.

But higher education institutions have made price far more complex by the way we use discounts, sometimes based on merit and sometimes based on need. To further confuse the issue, sometimes merit means academic achievement and sometime it means talent: talent in athletics, fine arts, etc. How we balance and calculate those various kinds of discounts are inconsistent, so no one knows what "sticker price" means or whether the discount offered is really a good deal. At some institutions, virtually no one pays the sticker price.

This situation has led to the public perception that higher education costs too much, no matter what institutions charge—despite the statement by the American Council on Education in 2009 that because of the diversity of institutions in the United States there is some college or university somewhere that virtually everyone can afford. When I try to explain this on Capitol Hill, the consistent response I get goes something like this: "That's nice, Mr. Lauer, but our constituents are telling us you cost too much and we are going to do something about it."

Accompanying the widespread (and incorrect) perception that higher education costs too much is a lack of understanding about the role it plays in the overall quality of life in America, in the economic development of our communities, and in the competiveness of our country around the world. These facts also are completely lost on the public today: that higher education is a labor-intensive effort, that top faculty must be paid, that keeping up with high technology is expensive, that utilities are skyrocketing, that maintenance of campus and buildings is never-ending and that most institutions are really pretty well-managed.

Recently, the U.S. Senate thought it would be possible to force universities to use a percentage of their endowment earnings to lower tuition. But university officers, like any other business officers, look at all their sources of income together, as well as all the expenses they are going to incur to do business, when they decide what they must spend and what they must charge. The fact that it is really impossible to use one source of income to lower price was completely lost on legislators. And the fact that big endowments are there to protect for a rainy day was lost too, until the economy went south along with many of the larger endowments.

So the most complex story we have to tell is about how we price and how we discount, and about the value that is received in exchange. And that story has to include messages about how everyone can find a place for a good education if they are flexible, realistic and investigate possibilities. Everyone on campus needs to understand this better so they can explain it better, and then take some responsibility for helping to educate the people they meet. Thus, price has become a major topic for the "learning organization" to address inside.

5. ORCHESTRATING A "TOTAL COLLEGE EXPERIENCE" IS THE KEY

The brand as the product is really about the total college experience, which is a blend of academic and college life and the way those experiential factors add up to knowing the character and values of the institution.

The residential college experience plays a major role in establishing a total collegiate lifestyle, which today will include choice of good housing, recreation facilities, quality and variety of food services, extracurricular options, leadership opportunities, Greek life, campus ambience, city amenities, job possibilities, career counseling and more. Providing and managing that total experience is what a competitive market requires, and so the learning that needs to take place includes understanding what makes up that experience at your institution and what it takes from everyone to deliver it. Remember the promise.

This branding principle even applies to distance learning. Distance learning is about convenience and the efficient delivery of information. It appeals to and satisfies a very specific market need, and its brand identity is established in the "how" of satisfying those distance and convenience needs. Indeed, they must be fulfilled at every step from inquiry, to application, to matriculation, to counseling, to taking the class, to evaluation, to graduation. There is a total college experience here, too, with a set of expectations based on the brand identity and market need.

This brings us to still another marketing and branding issue: retention. The typical reason people give when leaving a college or university is that their situation changed or they can no longer afford to stay. But the truth often is that the exchange of values is no longer valid for them: The brand promise, as they understood it, was not kept; they are no longer getting the value they expected for the price. Most prestigious schools have higher retention rates because the long-term value of the association with those institutions exists, even if the experience is disappointing. But for most of us, the brand value (i.e., total college experience) has to be delivered consistently and without exception.

6. THE ENTIRE STUDENT EXPERIENCE SHOULD BE "MAPPED"
Peter Slee, deputy vice-chancellor at the University of Huddersfield in the U.K., has been talking for sometime about mapping the student journey. Slee's term *mapping* applies the broadest definition possible to "the total college experience" by treating communicating student programming, the classroom experience, overall campus life and what happens after graduating as one long journey. It means charting it out as one integrated plan, and it asserts that one can actually integrate how and when communication (i.e., marketing) takes place throughout the entire journey.

Slee's approach could be a learning project for a university-wide marketing task force. Such a project would bring people from every corner of the campus together to see how everything they do all works together and to chart the experience for everyone to see. Such a chart could then become the foundation of a strategic plan, a fundraising plan and a master facility plan, since it would clearly show exactly what needs to take place when in order to realize the brand promise (and vision). This may sound a bit far-fetched at first, but the more you think about it, the more compelling it seems.

7. EFFECTIVE COMMUNICATION TODAY IS "MULTI-PLATFORM"
The days of mass communication are over. The idea that our work is merely sending out information is no longer sound. And most especially the thought that a primary objective of a communication office is to get our stories in the newspaper is long gone.

It might seem obvious to point out that the newspaper is no longer the primary source of information for the masses, but this fact does need to be said to many people in our institutions of higher education. They know about new media, but many continue to measure communication success by being able to cut out a story in the newspaper about their program. Therefore, you must take the time to demonstrate to the people you work with just what the consequences have been of this upheaval and rapid decline in the newspaper industry.

When communication professionals set out to communicate their organization and its programs today, they can no longer think primarily press releases and newspaper reporters. Even if they get a story in the newspaper, it's likely to be severely edited and buried, if it even runs at all, and few people will read it. So the professional now is more likely to first ask, "Who all needs to see this message?" and then, "What are the media of preference for that audience?" The answers to these questions today almost always involve direct and interactive new media.

Faculty, staff, students, alumni, donors and other opinion leaders need to come to understand that the whole communication business has changed dramatically and that the way the work is done is completely different. No longer is the press release the starting point. Instead, the direct media that are most likely to influence each target market segment are selected to produce a focused and intense impact. The objective is to cut through the clutter of today's information-saturated world by focusing essentially the same basic message points on top priority target markets. Consistency, repetition and interactivity are important success factors. Otherwise the message will be lost.

We call this "multi-platform" communication, and learning how to use it strategically is the foundation of educating today's communication practitioner. Today's communication professionals must master print, radio, television, the Internet, social media and special events. They need to know how to think differently, and so do our clients. They need to think about "convergence."

8. MARKETING REQUIRES "CONVERGENCE COMMUNICATION"

"Convergence" imagines the same message coming from a number of sources at both the same and different times to converge on each audience and each individual in the audience.

For example, an advertisement that makes the institution look impressive and exciting may appear in a magazine at pretty much the same time that a brochure arrives in the mail, about the same time that a telemarketing call comes in, at pretty much the same time the president appears on a radio or TV talk show, and so forth. Each message looks a bit different from the others and has slightly different content, but each also carries the brand identity and the same core message that differentiates the institution.

In other words, intensity is created by message consistency and by using a variety of the platforms selected from research that indicates they are the audience's preferred media. The intensity produced by convergence gets the message through the clutter and produces results. And since so many of the new media are interactive, the feedback and data collected allow the communication to turn into dialogue, or a least potential dialogue. This ongoing communication feels more like a conversation and thus over time magnifies and intensifies the convergence effect.

Over the course of a day, the professionals in communication offices will use a variety of media to focus the institution's messages on the markets that make the most difference to its future. The objective is not just to get the message through but also to build an ongoing relationship with the opinion leaders in each audience that quite literally can last a lifetime. It may not be important for all your clients to know all of this, but they certainly need to know the basics so they will have realistic expectations and will also appreciate what you know about communicating in today's world, and what they do not.

9. MEDIA PREFERENCES CHANGE WITH LIFE STAGES

Just as soon as you think you understand the media preferences for a particular market segment, they change. As people grow older and their circumstances change, their media behavior changes, too. And only asking people what they want does not always tell you how they actually behave. This, too, must be understood by clients for them to be able to fully appreciate what you do.

I learned about asking people what they want when I produced television programs years ago. People would say they were tired of seeing so much "junk" on television and that they wanted more serious programs. But when they came home after a hard day at work, they would watch the comedy that provided escape or the action drama that kept them on the edge of their seat or the football game that delivered color and excitement. And when they watched the news, the hard-hitting dramatic presentations—with fast-moving action and minimal information—would catch their attention. This was true for most people, children through older adults. There were always the exceptions, of course, but that's what they were: exceptions. Even public television found itself often walking a fine line between entertainment and serious information.

New media has brought with it a whole new set of media behavior factors, and those new behaviors appear to be changing at least every two years. New tactics become hot and others passé. Print continues to play a role, but it changes. Everything is different than it used to be. The one constant lesson of communications history, however, is that no medium has ever gone away completely. When the dominant medium changes because of advances in technology, the previous dominant medium changes roles, but it doesn't disappear. And all the others change roles, too.

So media preference analysis these days requires knowing that behaviors will be different at different life stages and expecting them to evolve and change within life stages, too. The only way to master the situation is to be active in the various media platforms all the time. This has become the responsibility of the communication professional and has greatly changed what we do with our time.

One benefit of this new technology is that its built-in feedback provides information about who is receiving what and how they feel about it. If you pay attention, that feedback can be the most reliable information you have.

10. NO ONE KNOWS WHERE THE NEWS BUSINESS IS HEADED

Sometimes I think the mystery about what the news business will settle into will sort itself out soon; but when I reflect on the nature of the high-speed digital technology we are dealing with, I realize that the business is capable of evolving into new forms and possibilities for a long time. What has been found only on a desktop moves to a laptop, and then moves to a mobile phone, and who knows where next. Computers and TV sets can be one and the same. What news is tracked through RSS feeds gives way, for many, to following favorite blogs. Others download podcasts to keep up.

We are in a "buyer beware" world of news. Many print and TV reporters still research and edit information with objectivity, but in more and more cases opinion is replacing hard facts, speed is replacing accuracy, confrontation is replacing civilized debate, argumentation is replacing courtesy, amateurs are taking the photos and humor has become a medium for conveying perceived truth.

Schools and universities, therefore, will need to spend more time educating their audience about how to consume media. Students will have to develop their own standards for making sure they stay informed about the world. They will have to become discerning critics and take responsibility for separating fact from fiction, truth from polarized extremes. When they program their daily intake of information they will have to be wise in their choices and not expect anyone else to be doing that for them.

So universities will be educating and training a whole new breed of multi-platform communicators to converge a variety of selected media on targeted market segments. They will be developing courses and other educational experiences that produce an educated and wise consumer of that media. And in addition, marketing and communication practitioners will have to educate those around us about the dramatic changes in how we communicate the institution as a result of these forces.

11. INTEGRATION IS THE KEY

In the new media world we talk about creating the "buzz." In the old media world we referred to the same thing as "word-of-mouth." In both media worlds, it is the most powerful form of communication. Generating the buzz through word-of-mouth is what we hope to accomplish as a result of our use of all other media.

The key to creating buzz is getting everyone on the same page. If you can get everyone to explain the competitive advantage of your institution in the same way and to be committed to telling the story, you have harnessed the most powerful tool in all of communication. The key is achieving the integration necessary to get everyone moving together in the same direction.

Integration is getting separate units to work together toward a common cause. People will need to get out of their "boxes," meet together and see how they can move ahead—together. It means, for example, discovering how admissions and marketing and communication can come together to plan visibility and recruiting initiatives that make a real difference.

Integration means finding and using talented people from all parts of the institution, whether or not they are in your area. Marketing and communicating takes place in all units, and in a university there are all levels of talent everywhere you look. Identifying that talent and mobilizing it is integration.

Likewise, money is spent on marketing and communication in every corner of the institution. When institutional marketing is planned through integrated processes, how that money is spent is influenced by those processes. Thus, with no budget increase at all, you are able to get more out of what is already being spent just by influencing others to spend their money in certain ways—ways that continue to benefit them, of course, but now also benefit the entire institution.

Integration also is multi-platform communication. It means sidestepping those old arguments about PR vs. advertising, or marketing vs. communications.

Today those arguments are irrelevant. One is not more powerful than the other. Rather, as we have argued, it's a matter of choosing the right tools at the right time to achieve a particular marketing goal. Presidents and CEOs don't care what it's called; they want results. And we do, too. Our professions have wasted too much time in the past specializing in media forms. Today everyone needs to know how to use all the tools in the toolbox.

In the final analysis, integration means that units of the institution move forward in the long term only if the institution is moving forward, too. When strategic planning, master planning, campaign planning and marketing and communications planning are all actually integrated, the institution becomes a true learning organization and everyone appreciates in a whole new way the power of what you do. But the internal education about all this must take place, and you are likely to have to be the one to orchestrate it.

12. TASK FORCES AND ACTION TEAMS ARE THE BASIC INTEGRATION TOOLS

The most efficient way to begin the integration of university marketing is to create a university-wide marketing task force. To be effective, the group should report to the president's office and be chaired by someone who can champion the cause.

Choosing the right champion is essential for success. This person must have the respect of both the faculty and the staff and must know the subject matter well enough to walk the talk, and teach it too. The person must believe in the power of communication to transform and must be persistent enough to press on when progress is slow.

The task force should be given the task of defining or clarifying the institution's competitive advantage and thus its brand. This can be done through a series of brainstorming groups, with the final objective of the task force to be the overseer of major initiative implementation.

The task force also becomes the place where people from all facets of the organization keep each other informed about what each is doing. As those conversations take place, common understandings develop. Over time, discussions move from central brand clarification, to sub-brand standards, to the development of special action initiatives for the institution as a whole.

Members of the task force will come from the schools and colleges, admissions, alumni relations, marketing and communications, athletics, student affairs and sometimes even the bookstore. They are selected because of their known interest in and or talent for marketing, and not just for their administrative position. They work as a team on the big-picture issues, but they also create other action teams to make special marketing initiatives happen.

Special initiatives are designed to create the perception that an institution is stepping out and moving forward. One central question for task force discussion should be: What two or three initiatives at this time and place will move us forward most effectively? Action teams can be appointed to plan and implement each initiative.

Each team will have a planner, designer, writer, sometimes an event person, a new media person and a researcher. The team will develop a plan and a budget and then seek support from the task force for implementation. The task force will see if the funds can be found from within existing budgets (and they often can) or will request new funds from the president and senior administration. While new money is not always available, the process approach will always establish a dynamic and a momentum that eventually achieves something new and significant.

Integration through task forces and teams is the most effective first step. In time some institutions will want to consider reorganization. Some will separate marketing and communications from fundraising and alumni relations; others put admissions and marketing and communications together. Still others make no changes. Every institution will have to use some kind of committee or task force approach to achieve the widespread integration necessary to get everyone on the same page and moving in the same direction.

The integration process, and the support for it at the top, is more important than the organizational structure. Understanding this requires educating the institution about it, and that will require your personal attention and initiative.

13. THE NATURE OF CREATIVITY

The capacity to remain creative and innovative is important for individuals and for teams in marketing and communication. In the course of a career, we go through periods when we feel creative ideas are flowing, and other periods when all creative instincts seem to have dried up forever. It is a frustrating reality of our profession. There are some times when our personal tastes connect with this or that market segment, and other times when our own judgments don't match the audience's at all. Research is essential for testing ideas, and it can help in generating them as well. But in the final analysis, creativity is not easily quantifiable, and you must find and implement the right processes for generating it.

The political challenge is to get your clients to understand that creativity is not thinking up cute things. Anyone can do that. It is a matter of selecting the right creative idea that connects in a compelling way with a market segment. This factor is what makes creativity a professional matter. Professionals use special skills and devices to generate and implement the right creative ideas for each task. Every client needs to understand the complexity of the creative process. It's not something that just anyone can do.

When a marketing and communication unit works in teams, approaching creativity professionally is its responsibility. Individual creativity contributes to the team, of course, but the group ultimately should deal with creativity as an interactive group process. How, then, should a team approach generating creative ideas? What are the tools they might employ? Again, this becomes a matter for "learning" in the learning organization.

An Internet search reveals that people study creativity as an academic subject. Not all you learn from these academic studies is applicable to your work, but you can begin to understand some basic concepts and learn about some creative processes and techniques that others have employed. In the end you will select the process or processes that best work for you. And after some experience, most groups conclude that they must periodically engage in some systematic creative idea generation activities.

I have identified four basic marketing situations where extra creativity is always needed: (1) generating a completely new "product" (which in this case applies more to a program or project idea for visibility than brand identity), (2) finding a new way to present the same thing, (3) producing a new look or design, (4) applying a new attitude, energy and tone to the overall marketing and communications initiative. This last one is intended to generate a "new day" feel to the organization and is often the focus of creative discussions.

One byproduct of introducing the study of creativity is the development of an overall entrepreneurial attitude in the group. Entrepreneurs are able to imagine things in completely new ways, see connections to market needs, are attracted to calculated risks and are able to talk easily about vision. They are inspirational in their language and demonstrate a commitment to hard work. They work right through their own fears and generate a look of self-confidence, even when they have some doubts. They bet on their calculation of risk and believe that taking this risk will push the action to success. In the final analysis, entrepreneurs know how to organize a plan of action and see having such a plan as a matter of strategic necessity. Therefore, they will work from a business plan that is simple, straightforward and easily described. They understand better than others how organizations get lost in their own complexity. They can maintain a simple focus while also tolerating and managing through constant ambiguity.

Developing these entrepreneurial qualities will prepare you for using your human and other resources skillfully and for facing the political realities ahead. Approaching your institution as if you were the entrepreneur that imagined its existence to begin with is a healthy way to begin a marketing initiative. This way, handling the politics will seem second nature, rather than being the part of the job that you hate.

Fostering creativity and innovation requires you to adopt some creative processes. Here are some that I have found useful. Through trial and error you may put together a slightly different list, but you can begin by considering these:

- **Group brainstorming.** This is the simple process of listing ideas until exhausted, and then systematically analyzing the pluses and minuses of each one. The final task is to put them in priority order until a decision for action is made.

- **Identifying creative clusters.** This is a form of benchmarking where you look at what others have done in a similar situation, analyze each example in light of your circumstances and then build your own idea out of the relevant elements.

- **Gathering in unconventional environments.** Different environments may suggest completely different approaches. A forest will suggest certain kinds of ideas, a factory still others, and a kindergarten room still another. Gathering in an art museum may be the best way to generate innovative thoughts for the fine arts school, but it also might work for an edgy approach to athletics.

- **Mind-stretching exercises.** The last example is related to this approach. Select a totally incompatible environment to push the group to completely new ideas, or give them an exercise to complete. For example, you might send your team to photograph, on their mobile phones, the most creative graffiti they can find in your city. They then return to present the photographs to the team, discussing how the images might influence the next advertising campaign, or why they will not.

- **Stream-of-consciousness tasks.** Ask some team members to keep a journal, others to carry a sketch pad around (depending on each individual's talent), to record their ideas for a prescribed period. At the next team meeting, they report what they have come up with. I have carried a notepad with me for years, making notes sometimes all day long. I have been an avid motorcyclist and always have taken a pad with me, often stopping to record ideas before I lose them. This is the way the books I have written are developed. For me, the journal has been the most effective tool I could have employed.

- **Adapting ideas from one form to another.** This is much like the other processes. It involves taking ideas from one medium or source and applying them to a completely different one. For example, apply a favorite painting to an ad design or an eye-catching print layout, then to a marketing publication.

It is important to note here that teams, like organizations, require both project and ongoing leadership. Marketing and communication campaigns themselves ebb and flow, gain visibility and then fade. But sustained growth requires leaders who make the processes ongoing, ever renewing by both keeping the team moving forward and walking the talk.

The work of the team must extend beyond itself. The ideas generated must also find their way into the "talk" of everyone, especially the executive leadership. This means that speeches must be compatible with campaigns: While constantly creative, they must also remain true to the brand identity.

Obviously, all these thoughts about creativity do not need to be taught to clients. All they need to know is that generating workable creative ideas is a matter of professional practice and not just thinking up cool ideas, and that the professionally determined creative approach needs to be consistently carried forward in how the messages are presented and how the talk is walked.

14. THE IMPORTANCE OF CO-BRANDS

While the institution has a brand identity, schools and colleges (and in some cases institutes and special programs) are co-brands. Shaping these co-brands effectively, and gaining the support and cooperation of deans and directors, is one of the most important tasks of the entire marketing and communication enterprise. Accomplishing this to everyone's satisfaction is the primary prerequisite for long-term institutional success in the marketplace.

A school or program has a legitimate claim for developing a co-brand identity if it has to connect to a specific market segment that has apparent and individual market expectations. For example, a business school should look like it means business; an engineering program should be and look high tech; a fine arts school should appear to be the cutting-edge leader of its world. But each of these, while maintaining its own look and consistency, should also carry the basic brand message and look of its institution. So the key is finding the formula for accomplishing both objectives.

Achieving this understanding throughout the leadership of the institution is a major educational challenge for the learning organization, and it requires a game plan and a good deal of savvy combined with persistence.

Most deans and some special program directors are hired much the same as presidents. They are told they are responsible for making the program successful by meeting admissions goals, raising money and building both visibility and reputation in the field. If the deans or directors are at all experienced, they will have the confidence that they can accomplish all this, and they will also resent someone from central administration telling them how they must present their program. Telling them they have branding restrictions and must clear what they do with a central authority will not go down well.

If the relationship with deans and directors is not managed skillfully, entrenched silos will form, and it's been my experience that in a fight the dean will win almost every time. Presidents or provosts will not intervene because their first commitment is to the academic leadership they put in place. In fact, I have known of several marketing and communications executives who have lost their jobs because the deans would not work with them. The "logo police" approach does not work. Wrong politics!

So again we have an education challenge. The key is to approach deans and special program directors by suggesting you will help develop a comprehensive plan that first and foremost will meet their program objectives. They must be assured that the design will make them proud in their marketplace and the message will differentiate their program, and that all this can also advance the institution's brand. They must be convinced or no progress will be made, either in your relationship or in the marketing.

There are a number of ways to go about this confidence-building education, but the one that works best for me is to describe the situation as an 85-15 formula. For example, let's suggest that about 85 percent of the program's basic general picture brochure will look the way the dean wants it to, and 15 percent will carry the institution's identity. The 15 percent can be simply a strip down the side, or it can be a more subtle approach, such as the use of color with an identity mark. Some solve the problem with a design symbol for the university appearing in the corner and a word-mark for the school or program at the top that incorporates the university symbol into a special font used only for this program. Making this work requires a cooperative attitude from the beginning, a trust that everyone's interests will be satisfied before anyone does anything, maximum flexibility within reason and creative people who grasp the concepts before they shape the words and design.

This last point is critically important. An important lesson learned over the years is that when designers and writers are a part of the whole process (i.e., present at and part of the birth of marketing ideas) their work invariably is right on target. When they are brought in too late, invariably people feel their work is off the mark. (The reasons for this are obvious. No further explanation needed.)

A co-brand is built using the same process as a brand. Groups within the school or program are formed, strengths and themes brainstormed and competitive advantage defined so that all understand. The institutional brand definition should be on the table throughout this process, however, so that participants are aware of it during their discussions. Ideally, the institution's marketing and communications executive or the chair of the marketing task force should facilitate those discussions.

15. INTERACTIVE COMMUNICATION AS RESEARCH

New media has brought a breakthrough in communication and marketing research. In the past we only knew about our audiences through surveys or interviews, both of which are costly. Now we can build feedback into the communication process, and as we learn to use it effectively it has the potential to be both a learning and budget breakthrough.

Surveys and interviews have limitations beyond the budgetary one. Many major, expensive surveys have yielded little useful information. They asked too many questions and tended to reinforce what you already knew. Few breakthrough marketing decisions have been driven by the results of big surveys.

Some of the more useful projects are the more focused ones that ask only a few questions about a specific decision to be made for a specific target market. I believe that many of these targeted surveys can eventually be replaced by the systematic feedback we can build into modern communication tactics.

When you send messages out and experience the feedback and consistency of results over time, you come to understand how to make decisions that are likely to work. And when you need new information to make a decision, you can usually get the information by asking a few specific questions to a particular market segment. Now, the new media communication process itself provides the feedback that you can then easily test through specific follow-up questions that your admissions or fundraising or alumni professionals pose to individuals and groups as they travel. While it might not be quite as controlled a situation as some quantitative projects, the information you get from this kind of feedback, when combined with your professional experience and judgment, is often reliable enough. The key to interpreting the information is to be working in the process on a daily basis, which most researchers are not.

The money that the new media is costing you might at least be partially offset by the research you will not have to do. Your clients need to understand this just enough to see and appreciate the professionalism of you and your staff. The learning organization will lead the others when everyone understands how powerful interactive communication can be, and teaching the leaders at your institution about that is part of the political strategy of gaining support for what you do.

16. TODAY'S PROFESSIONAL SHOULD FUNCTION LIKE AN ACCOUNT EXECUTIVE

It is a mistake to set up a communications office as the kind of service where people come to order work done. In the past, information offices and news services might have covered schools and program as "beats," giving the impression that you could bring the news to the communications office and tell the staff there what news releases to send out.

Brochures and other media were "ordered" in this manner as well. Someone from a school, academic program or other administrative department would show up in the communications office and say, "We need you to help write and produce a new flyer (or video or event) for us." The work of such an office became one of trying to meet perceived expectations, whether or not this project really was an institutional marketing priority. When caught up in this kind of service orientation, the office has little hope of providing marketing leadership and setting priorities.

Instead, the communications office should be seen as a group of professional marketing and communications consultants functioning more as internal account executives. You might have to modify the definition of the term *account executive* and adjust how the post functions to meet the reality of your situation, but ideally you would have enough "AEs" so that each one had only several internal "clients." Each AE would work with his or her clients to help design a comprehensive plan that would define each client's co-brand, tie it into the institutional brand, set clear targets and choose the tools in the communication toolbox appropriate to each priority target market. Potential news stories that enhance the brand identity would also be identified in this process, so realistic judgments could be made about placement potential in this 24-7 news world. And when it would be more effective to tell that story in more direct ways, those ways would be identified and put into the plan. Who would do what and when would be a shared decision.

Some of the work would be done by the sub-brand school or program staff (only where they had the internal expertise, of course), some by the central marketing and communication office and, at times, some by external or freelance help. Central office staff designers, writers and events processes would be managed by the account executive, who would also coordinate the work of everyone else to provide unity. Of course, where staff resources were too lean to make all this possible, a modified approach would have to be taken. But even in a very small office, the account executive model is a better way for the university to see marketing and communications professionals than in the more traditional role of service-on-demand providers.

Most likely you will have to teach this new approach to marketing. But the potential for improved results is so great that undertaking this teaching over time will ensure the client's support for what you as professionals do.

17. INTERNAL MARKETING AND INTERNAL COMMUNICATIONS ARE NOT THE SAME

Another part of what you must teach others at your institution is the difference between internal marketing and internal communications. Internal marketing is new to most institutions, and launching an internal initiative is essential to getting everyone on the same page.

Internal communications is the practice of keeping people informed about management decisions, the news of the day, institutional policies, special events, employee benefits, human interest stories about employees and their families and the critical and controversial issues affecting everyone's welfare. This is an important aspect of community building, and most institutions actually do a pretty poor job of it. Print and online newsletters, electronic message boards, radio and television are the traditional tools.

A university-wide marketing task force usually starts to be active after brand identity has been clarified and people are being asked to tell the story and walk the talk. There will need to be some way to get the campus informed and actively involved, and the tools for doing this may be quite new to most people.

All signage will eventually have to be made consistent with the brand. Banners inside and out are often used to add a touch of the right color and carry a few simple message points or the tag line. Briefings at staff meetings can be done by task force members. Presentations in new employee and faculty orientations (before they have a chance to become cynical) and the content of remarks at official events all can become vehicles for spreading the brand message. Such an internal marketing initiative has to be organized and managed over time. Therefore, the need for such an internal marketing initiative must be included as one of the teaching objectives of the marketing and communications professional.

18. THE ALUMNI PROGRAM IS SELF-PERPETUATING SECURITY

One of the most important political moves for a university marketing officer is to take the initiative to show alumni program leadership just how critical they are to the success of the entire institution, and then show them how marketing can help them expand their influence. Having accomplished that, the next step is to make sure that the leadership of the university is also educated about the potential that is right under their noses.

Using the power of strategic marketing planning to mobilize alumni to help find the best students, build prestige through word-of-mouth, raise money and become the hub that connects all living alumni to all facets of the institution for a lifetime should be a no-brainer for university leadership. But if the alumni program at your institution is in a "can't see the forest for the trees" situation, your job is to show everyone how the marketing staff can integrate with the alumni staff to mobilize this powerful future force.

In times when government roles are changing, funding sources are declining, investment yields are more questionable, student markets are more competitive and widespread visibility is harder to achieve, aggressively expanding the alumni relations program can be a very smart strategic move. Huge institutions that graduate thousands of students every year and have hundreds of thousands of alumni around the world especially have the potential to see their entire alumni body as a self-perpetuating marketplace. When properly planned, implemented and marketed, a broad-based alumni program can indeed help raise more money from more sources, recruit students in very personable and direct ways, help achieve more visibility in target locations, build reputation by walking the talk all over the world, and do all this by also maintaining lifetime connections with the entire university, no matter where alumni choose to live.

We have previously discussed how media preference changes with life stages. These life-cycle changes should be used as a planning and implementation framework in alumni programming and communication. The communication process should begin with initial contacts with prospective students, continue through the matriculation process, include making the most of the total university experience, and then move into the various life stages of the graduate right on through senior adulthood. These stages might be organized like this: (1) self-centered getting started years of the young alumni in their 20s, (2) young professionals developing their careers in their 30s, (3) alumni families expanding interests to include children and general enrichment in their 30s and 40s, (4) middle-age rethinking and growing, and (5) the many different life-changing and enrichment needs of the senior years. You might come up with a different set of categories. Meeting these needs during all of the stages has the potential to become the best future security your institution could hope to have. And so, an investment in making this kind of broad-based program happen might very well be the wisest investment your institution can make.

This kind of alumni program has to be a total-enterprise undertaking. It requires everyone to understand the institution as a lifelong resource for every person in it, and especially for every graduate of it. Everyone—faculty, staff, current students and alumni themselves—will have to take a role in making this program a reality. Just what are the elements of such a program?

- **Necessary technology** to get and maintain lifetime family connections. Make the website the initial point of contact so that the alumni come there first. From there, they can find anything they need from the total institution. The website is the portal to everything social and educational for the rest of their life.

- **Social and athletics events listings,** including instant access to reservations, tickets, payment mechanisms and guides to venues and related opportunities, made available on your website and through smart-phone apps.

- **Communities of interest** that offer real opportunities for people with all kinds of interests to interact and find a virtual and actual lifetime home with their university though the alumni association. The possible number and variety of these are is unlimited. In today's digital world these communities are most likely to begin as virtual, electronic communities from which a natural volunteer community organizer or two emerges. They then have the potential to morph into in-person meetings and experiences.

- **Continuing education,** from helping alumni keep up-to-date with their careers to retraining for a new vocation, from enrichment courses to other educational opportunities at alma mater (on campus or online). The website becomes the portal for information about all these opportunities. Graduates are reminded that the university is a lifetime career and educational resource for them.

- **Alumni travel,** for recreation and/or education. Travel study has been a longtime feature of alumni programs, but many programs are now finding that allowing alumni to enroll with current students in travel study courses enriches the experience for everyone, including the faculty.

- **A fundraising-friendly environment.** This broader context of involvement lessens the impression that some alumni develop that their university is always only asking them for money, and it allows an awareness of the importance of financial underwriting to develop more gradually and can nurture a heightened willingness to give back to the institution that is providing them so much.

- **More engaged in student recruitment.** By partnering with the admissions office, the alumni relations program can help organize sophisticated recruiting initiatives. There is nothing more powerful than successful alumni telling top high school seniors about the quality education and job opportunities that will come their way by attending and graduating from this university. This can even trump financial aid as a deciding factor in many situations. And combining the two will almost always be a sure winner.

- **Reputation is best built by word-of-mouth.** There is no doubt this just has to become a major initiative of any modern alumni program. There is no more effective marketing than having important opinion leaders walk the talk for you. Social media tools are high tech ways to launch and sustain a word-of-mouth campaign, and an alumni program is a natural place from which to organize such as effort. Give your alumni the message, motivate them with the vision and ask them to go tell the story. This can be done at live meetings and events, and it can be done by training volunteers to take your message points to the social media platforms they use. It's all a matter of teaching people about the possibilities, the technology and, where necessary, the techniques. Again, we reference your need to teach others about how this works in the learning organization.

Possibly we should be calling what we have been discussing "multi-platform alumni relations." It begins, as all marketing must, with brand clarification and thinks in terms of both virtual and actual lifelong connections.

19. A FRESH LOOK AT DONOR LOYALTY

Maintaining donor loyalty for the long term is also a matter for university-wide consideration. Intense competition for the philanthropic dollar challenges academic institutions as they undertake endless back-to-back campaigns. The political challenge here is to bring advancement and university officials to see how strategic marketing and creative thinking processes can effectively address the issue of maintaining donor loyalty.

Some advancement professionals and consultants maintain that back-to-back campaigns will continue to work forever, but with every nonprofit on the planet asking the same people for money over and over again, it's hard to believe that campaigns can be endlessly effective—unless we find new ways to engage donors. Everyone makes their best case and offers donors both honors and public recognition. Everyone uses gift levels and clubs, stages recognition events, offers naming opportunities and finds ways to give unique plaques, certificates and gifts. But will the effectiveness of all this come to a screeching halt? And if so, when?

In the past, most of us have felt that donors should be kept at arm's length from program involvement. Our attitude has developed pretty firmly that donor involvement in any aspect of operations is inappropriate and that giving them periodic public recognition is the proper way to make them feel good. "Keep them out of here," I heard one scientist say about his lab, and the thought has been articulated many times in regard to the classroom, academic offices, exhibitions, theater performances and almost every other facet of university life.

But aren't most people likely to give the most to what advances their passion? While public recognition is nice and important, especially at first, some sort of ongoing participation in the area of a person's passion seems likely to be more desirable in maintaining a donor's commitment. The long-term challenge might be to find appropriate ways to give donors an ongoing connection with their passion as a way of making them lifetime donors. And if this is so, strategic marketing can help find and lead the way. Making the case for marketing as a part of the integrated solution to this problem is your political challenge.

A major university in Canada is exploring the possibility of moving its advancement program away from back-to-back comprehensive campaigns into what it calls a sustained giving program by significantly increasing the annual fund goal, integrating all advancement areas to give more focus to building key relationships and finding new ways to increase donor opportunities for maintaining meaningful university connections. The university plans to achieve this by organizing all advancement under marketing. Small campaigns would continue to be launched for specific programs and faculties when needed, but the university-wide campaign would end.

Using this sustained-giving approach would end the staffing-up and budgeting-up for every comprehensive campaign, a process that requires taking on campaign-specific staff, producing new cases and materials, training staff and volunteers, gearing up the intensity of the moment, dismantling it all when the campaign is over—and then starting all over again for the new campaign. The challenge of a sustained-giving program would be to develop a permanent staff initiative that can reach larger annual goals, truly integrate the operation and not just talk about integration and then find those new and innovative ways to maintain donor loyalty. This last one might be the biggest challenge.

There is little doubt that finding ways for donors to become involved in what they fund is likely to be the largest "teaching" challenge of the whole sustained concept. Indeed, this is where everyone will have to play a role in the implementation, and many members of the faculty and staff will have to change years of thinking. How can we allow donors to participate in the passions they fund? Can they observe in labs? Are there special education events they can be a part of? Can they sit in classes? Can they sometimes lecture and/or participate in classroom discussions? Can they attend faculty and staff planning meetings; if so, is there an appropriate role for them to play? Can we define that role? Should they be encouraged to meet with student groups, and should we organize those opportunities for them?

These are the challenging questions we may have to address as we search for new ways to keep our donors loyal. Sustained-giving programs may be a reality of our future and therefore will become an additional education topic for the learning organization.

20. INTEGRATION WITH ATHLETICS

One large public university president told a group I was leading that he was trying to keep his athletics program brand separated from the university brand because athletics "did their own thing" and too often that "thing" was an embarrassment to the university. This, of course, was in response to my carefully articulated comments that integrating athletics and university marketing was an absolute necessity for maximum visibility and long-term success.

People very often tell me, "Athletics is over there and we are over here, and we have very little interaction." This sort of comment begs the question: "Well then, why do you have an athletics program to begin with? You are really two separate organizations."

The truth is, athletics brands and university brands can and must be integrated in order to justify having an athletics program at all. Athletics programs should be treated as sub-brands with the same claim to their own identity as the business school, for example, and the same responsibility to carry the university brand as well. Athletics should look like athletics but still look and sound like part of the parent institution. This is only a message and design issue that can be resolved through the kind of interaction and processes we have previously described as a part of ongoing integrated marketing practice.

Both athletics and the larger institution must have compatible values, purposes and messages. Integrated marketing finds ways both to show how athletics programs benefit the vitality of the campus and the community and to promote university programs and educational opportunities at athletics events. There is no doubt the two can and must be integrated; all it takes is the interactive processes described here and widespread task force–style participation.

Educating university faculty and staff about the positive potential of athletics can be challenging in some academic settings. But in every institution, I have found academics who love athletics and can be empowered to help tell that story. It just takes the right integrated process, an ongoing dialogue and advancement professionals accepting it as one of their educational and political challenges.

21. MARKETING PLANNING AND STRATEGIC PLANNING SHOULD BE THE SAME

Universities engage in strategic planning, master facilities planning, fundraising campaign planning and marketing/communications planning, and they are usually done at different times, unrelated to each other directly and often in an illogical order. There must be a better way.

Practice suggests that master plans are updated periodically at the initiative of the physical plant when it appears to people there that the plan is a bit out-dated. Fundraising campaign plans are undertaken when the administration and trustees decide it is time to raise money. Marketing plans come almost any time the need is felt to ratchet up visibility or enrollment. And the strategic plan is re-done at the initiative of a new president or when the need is felt to set fresh goals.

When you think of the process of overall planning, however, there is a natural order in which it should be done. The trend analysis parts of the strategic and marketing plans would be done first and simultaneously. This analysis would compare overall market trends, higher education market trends, trends in the job market and trends in higher education curriculum programming. The strategic plan would then compare the data to inherent institutional capacities and strengths in order to articulate a future vision and align needs and goals with market trends. The master plan would then be updated to provide for the plant and campus projects needed to support the goals of the strategic plan. Finally, the university would develop a fundraising plan to raise the money needed to support its goals and to meet related physical plant needs, which together would enable the institution to realize its vision.

It may just be wishful thinking that these plans would be developed in the right order at most academic institutions. But even if they are not actually done in the order I suggested, just realizing what the right order should be may help in reconciling them into some kind of integrated whole. Addressing the way these plans need to work together conceptually is an important exercise for the learning institution. This is a matter of fitting the pieces together and writing a report that shows how they integrate. And this can be a bringing-together activity of the marketing staff. Showing the potential of doing so is still another political objective and educational challenge for the marketing officer.

22. AND LEADERSHIP IS THE KEY TO IT ALL

It all comes down to leadership: accepting the leadership to educate the institution about how its industry is changing, developing the teams and processes necessary for getting people on the same page and helping the top executive realize just how critically important waking the talk will be to the whole marketing campaign.

There are many kinds of leadership styles, and we've discussed them in this book. In general, we all encounter some leaders who have just been put into or given their leadership role because of education or longevity or connections, and others who have earned it through years of hard work and commitment. Some leaders have been literally drafted by their followers, and some of these folks were clearly available and waiting while others were pushed reluctantly by supporters or events. Some are there because they have a special talent needed to handle a special situation and therefore are likely to falter if moved into another area of leadership (which often happens, to the detriment of that person and the institution).

Some leaders, as you recall, become autocrats, while others are facilitative and process oriented. The autocrats are so by nature or become so as a way of covering up their terrifying lack of self-confidence, which of course they discover on the job and often will not admit, even to themselves. The facilitator is the type of leader we hope to find, the one who is really needed at all levels to design the processes and be a lead teacher in the learning organization.

The facilitator listens first, and then acts. She or he admits mistakes but keeps going. Facilitators seek partnerships, take calculated risks and refer constantly to mission and vision. A passion for the business of higher education is evident in their demeanor, and they have a clear ability to see marketing as a total organizational responsibility. Facilitators inspire creative people, love to be around them and celebrate their talent. They are process people who do not see meeting and discussing as a waste of time, but rather as the main mechanism for moving the train down the track.

This type of leader uses planning task forces effectively, forms action teams to make significant things happen, facilitates setting priorities to keep everyone on course and sees and articulates brand identity and competitive advantage in visionary terms. This is the type of leader for whom you hope to be working, the type you are trying to teach and develop in the learning organization and the type you must strive to be yourself. In the final analysis, this type of leader has learned to love the politics because politics is at least half the job.

PART III

BEYOND THE ACADEMY

CHAPTER 8

Developing Support for the Greater Good

SO FAR, this book has been mostly about internal institutional politics and understanding how to deal with them. But universities exist in a highly political world outside their campuses, too. As university advancement professions are become more prominent in their institutions as a consequence of intense global competition, so marketing professionals will be more involved in the external political world. So now let's examine the political realities we face outside of academia.

THE PUBLIC NO LONGER UNDERSTANDS THE GREATER GOOD

Many colleagues now feel that the feedback they get from research and interactive media indicates that while the public in general understands the value of an individual college education, they no longer appreciate the larger role universities play in the overall quality of American life. My sense is that this may be gradually happening around the world as well. This is a serious issue.

If unchecked, this growing problem will have enormous consequences. When the larger roles that universities play are no longer comprehended or even publicly discussed, legislators stop seeing their increasing support as a top priority, city leaders lose sight of the importance of their local universities to their common future and people in greater numbers begin to express dissatisfaction with what they now perceive to be wasted overhead and inefficiency. As a consequence, society overall loses its sense that a learned community is the pathway to continued and growing social well-being.

While we acknowledge that people in general tend to see their own education as valuable, even that attitude is being questioned by many, based mainly on concerns about cost-benefit. In other words, people are beginning to calculate the total personal cost of their education in light of what they might expect to earn in a lifetime, both with and without a degree. This type of calculation puts a college education squarely in the category of producing a financial advantage.

Many people have lost the understanding that education is a pathway to much more than financial success. The notion that appreciating great literature and art, understanding the world of fine music and being able to comprehend and appreciate abstract ideas about life and religion and more is disappearing from today's discourse, or so it seems to me and many colleagues. What is the long-term consequence of such a loss to any society that considers itself superior?

Universities exist not only to teach, but also to discover new knowledge. Research is a fundamental role of academic institutions, and the education and maintenance of the scholars necessary for such discoveries is what accounts for much of the cost associated with running these institutions. Universities educate people who can both teach and find new information and then point the way to a better future for all of us. (There is little doubt that most of the work that will solve today's energy problems, for example, will begin in universities.) We need to do a much better job of making the significance of this enterprise better and more widely understood.

In addition, the research sponsored by universities is responsible for the discovery of many new products and services. It seems so obvious that our quality of life depends in large measure on these discoveries. Just as important, however, is how much industry depends on these discoveries as well. True, many companies have their own research and development operations, but equally true is that many of the fundamental ideas and product prototypes that result in new manufacturing opportunities begin in university laboratories.

The fact that both undergraduate and graduate students will study in this environment of research and discovery is critical to their understanding of their role as future leaders. This is a fundamental aspect of higher education: taking classes with scholars who put ideas and information in perspective while also exposing students to the excitement of discovering new knowledge. Much more effort needs to be focused on communicating this fact.

Universities also play an important economic role in their local and regional communities. In many places, universities are the largest employers, providing jobs for area residents; additionally, university employees (and students) spend their money in the community. The economic impact that most universities have on their communities is enormous and must be taken into account when calculating the overall cost-benefit to society. We need to talk much more about our industry as an economy driver.

Last but not least is the incredible role American higher education plays in our overall country's competitiveness around the world. The fact that we have been the go-to place for people all over the world who want an education that prepares them for leadership back in their home country is of no small significance. The only way to maintain this leadership role is to keep investing in the enterprise. This is especially true now as other countries make significant investments in their own systems. China has identified several institutions to become world-class in order to keep more of their best talent studying at home. India is doing the same thing.

Perhaps the United States will not be able to maintain the dominance in higher education that it currently enjoys, but we certainly can remain close to the top if we continue to invest in it. But such investment means more than providing classes for people to get degrees to get better jobs. It also means understanding the dimensions of greater good offered by our industry and communicating them with more vigor. It means insisting that we make the investment necessary to instill the joy of the world of ideas as well as provide careers and to continue the discovery of new knowledge through world-class research programs. And it also means recognizing the incredible economic development impact of universities, as well as the major role they play in maintaining the United States as a world leader and leading economic competitor.

EDUCATING ON THE ISSUES

In order to recapture the respect of legislators, as well as their financial support, it's important for more advocates for higher education to show up on Capitol Hill to tell our story. We might go there to talk about a specific piece of legislation, but it's essential that we tell the whole greater-good story before we leave.

In the past, I thought that a medium-sized private university like mine would have little influence in Washington. But recently I made my first trip to Congress and found not only that I was well-received but also that the legislators were genuinely interested in hearing from an institution they regarded as more representative of the majority around the country than those major ones that constantly camp out on Capitol Hill. I realized that people at many smaller institutions must be feeling like I did: that we would not have any influence and that taking time to visit Washington politicians would be a waste of our institutions' valuable resources. I found, however, that the politicians listened to what I said about the issues and were interested in what our institutions might have to say. At the end of the day, I was also able to lift the visibility and even the reputation of my institution just by being there.

The visibility alone had additional benefits. Over time my institution became better known in Washington and expanded its academic presence there, too. People in the legislature and their staff have children, relatives and friends, too. The better we got to know the legislative staff, the more they were telling others about us. In other words, these legislative initiatives yielded word-of-mouth, reputation-building and admissions results. In the process, we also learned of some project-funding possibilities we had not known about before.

The big legislative issues surrounding higher education are always cost and financial aid. Legislators hear from their constituents that higher education costs too much, and we tell those same legislators that we need more financial aid to do something about it. Legislators want to tell their constituents that they are passing legislation to hold down the cost of higher education, and then they look for an easy way to force that to happen—without considering the complexity of the higher education industry.

Our task is to find some way to help them understand that complexity. We need to "educate the legislature" as part of making a solid case for the greater good of higher education. Only when legislators understand all income sources, necessary expenses and management processes wrapped up in higher education can the cost issue be realistically addressed. Make no mistake about it: There is an important continuing role for government is this enterprise. Its support—for projects, research, special programs and need-based financial aid—is critical to keeping the entire industry viable.

It is especially important for us to counteract the perception among many legislators, their staffs and even the public that we are hiding our numbers and do not want anyone to know how we operate. Some even believe that we are afraid too much transparency will reveal how badly we are managed.

Unfortunately, too many people, including politicians, tend to see institutions of higher education as being all alike. They believe we are all unaccountable, inefficient and wasteful. They believe that every manager in higher education is inept. But just as in any other industry, some institutions are well-managed, others less so and a few should no doubt go away.

Additionally, the United States has a great variety of types of institutions: major research institutions, regional institutions, comprehensive private universities, small liberal arts colleges, religiously affiliated institutions, fine arts conservatories, community colleges and more. Each type has its unique distinctions, financial structures and markets. Some are higher priced, others are not. Somewhere there is an institution to which virtually anyone can find access, no matter what their financial or even academic situation. But even so, legislators continue to see us all alike: too expensive and mismanaged.

A major recent example is the issue of endowment spending. Legislators and staff on the U.S. Senate Finance Committee thought it would be possible to force universities with a certain size endowment to spend 5 percent of endowment earnings each year and to use those earnings to hold down tuition rates. This thinking was based on the huge endowments that a few elite universities had managed to build. But universities with endowments of a billion dollars or more often have annual budgets of at least one-third of that—which means that they only have three years of operations in the bank. That cushion can dwindle quickly, as it has in this most recent economic downturn.

And of course there is the matter of how annual budgets need to be put together as well. Simply put, you look at all your income and all your expenses, and then set your price with that and your marketing realities in mind. Some years you might be able to hold down tuition. But chances are with utilities going up, the cost of library acquisitions increasing, salaries requiring adjustments and roofs and buildings needing repair, you cannot always hold tuition down. And this does not even take into account the need for improvements to the physical plant as well as to the overall quality of the educational experience and programs. And so keeping down costs is a complicated challenge that only institutions working together with legislators can realistically find ways to do.

The bottom line is that more advancement professionals, especially those in marketing and communication, need to show up in the legislative arena and champion the greater-good message. Knowing how to use external political strategies and tactics effectively needs to become part of our training and our work.

WHAT STRATEGIC MARKETING CAN DO

The same strategies and tactics we use on our campuses apply when dealing with legislatures. The task is to mobilize the troops—your alumni, your donors, your trustees and your friendly politicians—to help tell the greater-good story. You need word-of-mouth buzz, and your tactics are the usual ones.

But with legislators, you have to formulate and promote a brand identity for the total higher education industry. In the case of individual institutions, the brand is based on how we do what we do, and we differentiate it from others to achieve our competitive advantage. So how do we define an industry brand?

It's pretty clear by now that I think the industry brand theme would probably be "Education for the greater good" and that the elements are individual advanced education, new knowledge and products discovery, expanded local economies and guaranteed world competitiveness. Now you put together the marketing initiatives for the industry pretty much as you do for your institution.

First you add the industry brand to your president's speeches. This is critical to starting the buzz and to establishing your institution as a leader in the industry. Once the message becomes a part of the president's talk, then you ask all other leaders, inside and out, professional and volunteer, to walk that same talk.

Now you take the same multi-platform, interactive media approach to planning your communication assault as you do for other marketing initiatives. You segment your audiences, find out their media preferences and employ interactive communication tactics using the audience's preferred tools. You note their feedback and then respond. In the case of legislators, you can segment them in many ways (i.e., by geography, by their perceived ability to influence, by the committees on which they serve, by how close they are to you, etc.). Then you combine your communications with personal calls from time to time and invitations to events. The key here, as in all other marketing these days, is engaging in interactive relationship-building and stressing the brand of the industry and the brand of the university over and over again.

You can also extend an explanation of what you are doing to other groups. For example, let voters in your constituency hear you communicate the greater-good benefits and the stand you are taking on issues. Tell faculty and staff and inform students and parents about your initiatives to reinforce their perception of you and their institution as a leader in its field.

And key among these external groups are your alumni—your most powerful force.

Alumni program executives will have to see all of the institution's alumni as lifelong learners, as reputation builders, as admissions recruiters, as fund-raisers and as lobbyists, and in so doing they will help shape the future of their institutions. Further, marketing professionals will need to share this vision of alumni involvement and work closely with these programs to advance both their institution and their industry.

ADVANCING ADVANCEMENT

In order for the advancement professions to step up to the challenge of this new day of global competition, practitioners will have to stretch beyond current development strategies and tactics and learn more about the issues shaping their industry as a whole. This is the difference between mere professional practice and institutional and industry leadership.

Most advancement conferences seem to focus mostly on fundraising, marketing, communication, and alumni relations strategies and tactics. The exception is the annual CASE Summit for Advancement Leaders. This meeting of the profession's leadership has attempted to put on the agenda the industry's critical issues, rather than just advancement topics, and invite leaders from all segments of higher education to examine them together. It seems to me the Summit's real purposes are to:

- Visibly associate advancement professionals with the presidents, deans, provosts, trustees, consultants, legislators, businessmen, journalists, new media gurus and all the others who are the idea people leading our industry; and

- Immerse advancement professionals in the big education and social issues they will need to deal with and communicate about so as to enable them to become leaders on their executive teams, in their professions and in higher education as a whole.

There is little doubt that the competition for students, money and reputation, coupled with the stresses of government cutbacks and worldwide economic trouble, have put the advancement professions front and center in determining the future of their institutions and now the future of the higher education industry as well. Thus the day has come for the advancement practitioner to become a full player on the strategic planning team. But being on that team will mean that each and every one of us will have to step up to the plate, learn about all the critical issues and be ready to teach the rest of the world about the greater good of higher education.

CHAPTER 9

The Challenge Ahead

WE BEGAN WITH THE ADMONITION that not only will you have to deal with institutional politics in the advancement profession, but that it's best if you can learn to love it. You can count on at least 50 percent of your time being spent on politics, so the more you can learn to like it, the happier you are likely to be.

My need to write this book was driven by hearing repeated references, at many conferences, to the pain of institutional politics. As I reflected on the frequency and depth of the concern, I realized that "politics" is rarely taught as a subject matter but that it might be possible to do so. And so I wrote this book.

In closing, I leave you with a basic summary of the subject of politics, as we've discussed here. By reviewing these basic points you will recall what you have read and be able to put it in a simple framework for your own application.

UNIVERSITIES ARE DIFFERENT

We all agree that universities could benefit from being more business-like, but they are not businesses. They are more like small-cities than anything else, and leading them involves both management and politics. Here are some of their characteristics.

1. Presidents have some administrative staff they manage but must use political influence with the others.

2. Faculty see themselves as free agents and go through various stages from untenured to tenured, with each stage having different behavior characteristics. You must understand each stage to be able to work effectively with faculty members.

3. Each institution is at a different stage in its historical development, and while all institutions may seem to be all alike, they are not. You need to understand the dynamics of the moment.

4. There are dramatic differences in academic leadership styles, depending on the experience of the individual in the position. Each style requires you to take a different approach.

5. Something about the nature of universities causes many academics to have an aversion to marketing, but it's because they do not understand that marketing is only a way of thinking. They just need to be educated—carefully—about what marketing is.

ORGANIZATIONS CHANGE PEOPLE

Being given responsibility for the first time can have a surprising effect on people. Some otherwise nice people become autocrats, while others become effective managers. All new leaders find that relationships with people around them change. Here are some of the change characteristics.

1. They become paranoid, developing feelings that people around them are undermining their effectiveness and affecting their security.

2. They find they are completely unprepared for their new responsibilities and try to compensate by becoming overbearing or by retreating into indecision.

3. They find that everyone now relates to them differently. Many old friendships end, some become adversarial, and new relationships form.

4. Because of insecurities, some hide behind excuses or fabricate complicated reasons for inaction.

5. Some want to look efficient and say "I will take care of it," and then do nothing.

6. Some bosses feel threatened by talented people around them, which requires some serious strategic thinking and planning if one of those talented people is you.

Organizations change people. Sometimes it's difficult to understand why, but it's a fact that requires you to analyze leadership and staff behaviors and develop political strategies and tactics accordingly.

A FEW BASIC POLITICAL TOOLS WILL SAVE THE DAY

With so much time devoted to politics in organizations, it seems appropriate to identify the tools most essential to help you get things done. Here are the basic ones.

1. Process tools or groups, including account executives to work with academic and other programs, task forces to coordinate thinking, action teams to launch initiatives, editorial priorities committees to reinforce brand characteristics.

2. Grass-roots political tools, such as dividing the institution into supporters, detractors and neutrals, and dealing with each separately.

There are also a number of typical political realities that will need to be addressed with one or more of these tools. They include:

1. The tendency for issues to get polarized;

2. The tendency for people to be either numbers or creative concept oriented;

3. The need to have a "seat" at the table, even if it's your representative;

4. The fact that talented people are often ignored or even ridiculed on their home turf;

5. The fact the most people feel insecure when leadership changes;

6. A major concern that some failures will cost you your job;

7. Your efforts to promote others may cause some to think you are manipulating them, or pushing them too aggressively, or actually just promoting yourself; and

8. The disappointment and frustration that your efforts to help someone advance to a new level was greeted by that person not being willing to step up.

Once you realize that it's part of your job to consciously analyze the nature of your institution and the players who are its leaders, and then to develop strategies and tactics to deal with the issues you face, it's a matter of a little practice to become proficient. Difficulty comes when your tendency is to say "I hate the politics." Happiness, however, will require you to enjoy the political challenge of making exciting things happen.

BE PREPARED TO BECOME A TEACHER

People in institutions generally misunderstand what marketing is all about. Either they think it's just a set of activities that anyone can think up and do, or they think it's commercializing a product or idea that will sell itself if it's just good enough (i.e., build it and they will come). After years of dealing with these misconceptions, I accepted that there was no way out of teaching everyone I could about what marketing really is and how professionals really work.

So developing a lesson plan for teaching key unit heads and opinion leaders the basics of marketing must become part of the institutional marketing and communication professional's job. Developing such a plan involves listing the most important basic concepts and clustering them under topic modules. Then you can conduct most of your marketing planning meetings by first taking a few minutes to "teach" one of the topic modules. Over time the participants learn the basic subject matter. This same approach can be taken in one-on-one meetings with deans and other unit heads in the institution. Here is a quick summary of what I think we want them to know.

1. Your main product is your brand.

2. An academic brand is a collection of unique benefits or features.

3. You reinforce the brand through editorial priorities.

4. Price is part of the brand and is the most complex story we have to explain.

5. Orchestrating a "total college experience" message is the key.

6. The entire student experience can be "mapped" from first contact to older alumni in order to clarify competitive advantage and brand, coordinate academic with student activities and enhance marketing initiatives.

7. Effective communication today is "multi-platform" and has little to do with the news media.

8. Several media are used simultaneously to "converge" on a specific market segment.

9. Media preferences change with life stages.

10. The future of the news business is uncertain, but marketing communication does not depend on it.

11. Integration of people, processes, media and messages creates the dynamics that move institutions ahead.

12. Institution-wide task forces and specific initiative action teams are the basic integration tools.

13. Developing systems for generating creative ideas is a management function.

14. Schools, colleges and some special programs are co-brands and must have their own distinction while also advancing the main brand.

15. Interactive communication is also feedback research.

16. An in-house agency approach with account executives working with internal units to develop comprehensive plans is an effective way to operate a marketing and communication program.

17. Internal communication is keeping people informed, and internal marketing is getting people on the same page with regard to brand identity and competitive advantage.

18. A broad-based alumni program is self-perpetuating security.

19. Donor loyalty will be the future fundraising challenge, and marketing can provide some solutions.

20. Athletics must advance the institutional brand; otherwise, what's the justification for the program?

21. The strategic plan and the marketing plan should be one and the same thing.

22. Out front, articulate leadership walking the right talk is the primary key to success.

Develop your own list from this one, and then cluster the points into modules that make sense to you. You will have to "own" your own subject matter in order to be convincing and to present it in a style that is comfortable to you. Some will prefer to use simple visuals and others will rather just talk through the concepts informally. But either way, make it clear that you are taking a few minutes to demonstrate the kind of thinking and sophistication required for understanding professional marketing. This will work well in group or one-on-one meetings once you have become practiced at making it seem natural.

PROMOTING THE GREATER GOOD

While this book focuses primarily on internal institutional politics, there is a growing need to get involved in external politics as well. This need stems from the realization that while people understand the value of getting a college degree, they also have forgotten the "greater good" qualities of higher education that make it important to society as a whole and justify the public's investment in it.

FORGOTTEN QUALITIES

Research and public feedback tell us that people no longer see the big picture when it comes to higher education. These larger values and forgotten qualities are the ones that make the public's investment in the enterprise an imperative.

1. Besides teaching students, universities discover new knowledge and do the research necessary to develop new products and human services.

2. University staff, faculty and students are major economic factors in their local areas and regions. They spend their money there and provide the educated expertise necessary to make the region prosper.

3. Universities are global enterprises and provide the intellectual capital essential to maintaining American competitiveness in the world.

LEGISLATIVE RELATIONS

It's not just the general public who is losing sight of the greater good of higher education. Legislators are finding it popular as well to criticize institutions with charges of inflated tuition and inefficient management. In an atmosphere of criticism and during a time of economic stress, it's all too easy to see cutting back on support as a feasible move. Here are the main issues that we need to address.

1. The perception that tuition is too high, even though there is little or no understanding in the legislature of what it costs to support both teaching and research in a small city.

2. The need for more financial aid, since costs are high even in well-managed institutions. Additional financial aid is the only way to maintain broad and fair access.

3. The public and legislators tend to see all colleges and universities as being all alike. They fail to see the distinctions of individual institutions, and they tend to assume we all are poorly managed and are wasting resources.

THE IMPORTANT NEED TO ADVANCE ADVANCEMENT

With most governments pulling back and tuitions increasing, advancement offices are coming to the forefront of their institutions. Suddenly there is intense interest in better legislative relations, more efficient fundraising, a more sophisticated alumni program and the strategic and integrated marketing that is the foundation of it all.

But to step up to meet those needs, advancement professionals must also be able to lead with the people at the top. That means we need to learn about all the issues shaping this industry and become active participants in all the dimensions of forging a new day. To do this we will need to enhance our own professional development. In addition to the strategies and tactics of the traditional advancement professions, we will need to study and become more sophisticated in organizational politics, governmental and legislative relations, and the social and other issues that affect our future.

The world is in turmoil; political and religious differences are tearing us apart. These problems can be solved in part through the soft-power gatherings of professors and students around the world and through the education and development of a whole new breed of global leader. These initiatives will come from higher education, if they are to come at all. And our universities will only be there if marketing and other advancement professionals are sophisticated enough to offer the needed support and necessary resources.

⇒◀ INDEX ▶⇐

fundraising
  alumni and, 109
  athletics and, 17
  building booms and, 16
  faculty's role in, 10, 11
  in international education, 73–74, 76
  mapping student experience, 93
  by public universities, 72
  relationship builder leadership and, 23
  strategic planning and, 113
  third-party advocates and, 46
future challenges, 127–33
  advancement and, 133
  forgotten qualities, 132
  greater good, promotion of, 132
  legislative relations, 132–33
  organizations change people, 128
  political tools and, 129
  teacher, preparedness to become,
    130–31
  universities are different, 127–28

G
government roles in international
  education, 70–71, 76
grass-roots political tools, 43–46, 129
greater good, support for, 119–25
  advancement and, 125
  educating on issues, 121–23
  as future challenge, 132
  public's understanding of, 119–21, 132
  strategic marketing in, 123–25

H
Harvard University, 75
heroes, making others, 37, 52–53, 129
How to Create Uncontested Market Space
  and Make the Competition Irrelevant
  (Kim & Mauborgne), 90

I
India, world-class education in, 121
Indian Business School, 75
information clutter, 4, 90, 94
INSEAD, 75
institutional culture, 14, 17, 60
integrated marketing, 87–115. See also
  marketing and communication
  academic brand as collection of
    benefits, 89–90
  account executives in, 105–6
  alumni programs in, 107–10, 131
  athletics in, 112-13, 131
  brand as main product, 88–89
  buzz, key to creating, 97–98
  co-brand importance, 102–4
  convergence communication, 94–95,
    130
  creativity in, 99–102, 131
  donor loyalty in, 110–12, 131
  editorial priorities and brand
    reinforcement, 90
  internal marketing vs. internal
    communication, 106–7, 131
  leadership role in, 114–15, 131
  mapping student experience, 93, 130
  media preferences and, 95–96, 130
  multi-platform communication,
    93–94, 97, 110, 124, 130
  news business and, 96–97, 130
  price, importance of, 91–92
  research, interactive communication
    as, 104–5
  strategic planning in, 112–13, 131
  task forces and action teams in,
    98–99, 131
  total college experience, 92–93
international education, 3, 69–76
  advancement professions role in, 76
  fundraising in, 73–74, 76
  government roles in, 70–71, 76
  public and private systems, 71–73
  student recruiting in, 74–76

⇒◄ ABOUT THE AUTHOR ►⇐

LARRY D. LAUER became Texas Christian University's first vice chancellor for government affairs in 2009. He is also distinguished professor of strategic communication at TCU's Schieffer School of Journalism and an adjunct fellow at the Center for Strategic and International Studies (CSIS) in Washington, D.C.

From 1999 to 2009 Lauer served as TCU's first vice chancellor for marketing and communication, and he directed the Commission on the Future of TCU, its strategic planning initiative, in 2000. He joined the TCU faculty in 1966, earned tenure in 1972, and became head of the evening college, the summer school and all noncredit programs in 1974. He began 30 years of directing TCU's communications and marketing programs in 1979, which included adapting the field of integrated marketing to higher education, teaching media studies, teaching strategic and international communication, public broadcasting projects and international education.

He is the author of *Communication Power* (Jones & Bartlett, 1997), *Competing for Students, Money and Reputation: Marketing the Academy in the 21st Century* (CASE, 2002), *Advancing Higher Education in Uncertain Times* (CASE, 2006), and more than 30 journal articles and book chapters on integrated marketing and communication. He edited the section on marketing in the third edition of the *CASE Handbook of Institutional Advancement*, (3rd ed.; CASE 2002), where he is referred to as "pioneer of integrated marketing for our profession."

Lauer received CASE's Alice L. Beeman Award for Research in Communication in 2003 and in 2007 (the only person to have received the award twice); the President's Award from Independent Colleges and Universities of Texas (ICUT) in 2003; and the Distinguished Achievement Award from CASE District IV in 2004.

Lauer was founding chairman of the CASE Advanced Seminar on Integrated Marketing and the redesigned CASE Summit for Advancement Leaders. He served on the advisory board of the American Council on Education's (ACE) Solutions for America project. He has been a faculty member and past chair of the CASE Summer Institutes on Communications and Marketing at Duke and Vanderbilt Universities.

Lauer speaks at national and international conferences, counsels with associations and has worked with more than 40 campuses on integrated marketing and strategic communication initiatives in the United States, Canada, Mexico, Chile, Columbia, South Africa, the Caribbean, the U.K., Poland, France, Italy, Germany, Spain, Australia, Denmark, the Netherlands and Singapore. He has presented papers at countless regional, national and international conferences.